Living With OCD

Living With OCD

Rajah Khetarpal

Order this book online at www.trafford.com
or email orders@trafford.com

Most Trafford titles are also available at major online book retailers.

Printed in the United States of America.

ISBN: 978-1-4269-4492-5 (sc)
ISBN: 978-1-4269-4493-2 (hc)
ISBN: 978-1-4269-4494-9 (e)

Library of Congress Control Number: 2010915625

Our mission is to efficiently provide the world's finest, most comprehensive book publishing service, enabling every author to experience success. To find out how to publish your book, your way, and have it available worldwide, visit us online at www.trafford.com

Trafford rev. 10/26/2010

 www.trafford.com

North America & international
toll-free: 1 888 232 4444 (USA & Canada)
phone: 250 383 6864 ♦ fax: 812 355 4082

12-30-2008

I am so lost. I can't think of any more drivel to write down. I feel a lot of my passion for life is erased never to return. What do I have to offer? What can I do to change this? All of this. I feel anxiety about death. I feel that my extreme **obsessive-compulsive disorder** is a heavy burden on my life. My soul is alive but weak. I waste a lot of time. I'm going nowhere really. How can I feel different? I want to feel a new purpose arise. Something much better. It's not about the girl, or honor, or anything else that I have lost. I have what is important to me and that is what really counts. I have my family. I have my existence; my life. I have to change a part of me that has been untouched; that I have not yet reached. This part of me has got to grow bigger and stronger and suck me into its everlasting, glorious power. My spirit is alive and is my only prayer. My spirit can take me far. I feel that my spirit is my guide.

I am incredibly lonely despite my large, beautiful family. I always have hate for myself. Always…Even when I am happy. This is so embarrassing and hard to write down. I am ashamed of myself to myself. This has all been written down before but by different people or by me at different periods in my life. It is very cliché. But is that why I feel ashamed and embarrassed to write this all down? I can lie to myself and say that all great thinkers and wise men write these self-deprecating words down from time to time. Hell, maybe they do. How boring of me to question myself so much. How selfish. All of the above.

Is it a good time to live? It is always a great time to live if we are blessed with life. To have it taken away…my God! To be alive you have to be brave. To live knowing one will ultimately die takes strength. We are all strong in our own ways. I concentrate too much on my weaknesses; however I believe that most of us do.

When is it a good time to be honest with another human? There are so many different degrees of honesty. Who knows?

The reason I am writing all of this down is to make myself feel better. I am writing too free myself; to free my soul. It feels so good to put some of this negativity from my head onto paper. I am cleansing my brain of its awful, nasty energy and cells. There is a science to this all. An art to this healing. This is what it takes to get better. Understand the science and art of healing the mind, body, and soul. Do not be too shy to accept the greatness and importance of this challenge. Another fight to stay alive. Alive and well.

I have failed before, and I'll probably fail again. But I will fight on again. Boy have I failed hard. Really, really hard. I have tried to forget but I cannot. Bad memories remain. My only hope is to forgive. To hell with this system of mine! The system of my life is hell! I quit it! I quit it now! Maybe I'll go back and have to quit it again. I'll try not to go back, but again: I have failed before.

Back to the science and art of healing. It is nature. It is all nature. Everything about me is all natural. Keep it this way. Don't let it get twisted. Do not let nature harm your own self. That is no good; unacceptable. Painful. I must let nature heal me. Nature loves to heal. I must go with it into a positive, exciting environment created naturally by myself. I am obviously the key to it all. I am also the lock. I can figure out how to open up into a miracle. Being alive alone is my right into being a miracle. That is no lie.

I can change a lot more. Everything I do day to day. Every intention possible. I am a good human. I just need to be better! It is so easy to forget and to take life for granted. It is easy to take breaths for granted. Does God remind me of this? What reminds me of this?

1-7-09

I am carrying this huge weight around with me. It is a heavy burden to feel no purpose and to feel worthless on most days. Some days I feel better but usually its shit. Same shit too. I feel that the past has been such a bad trip and that I cannot escape it. It lingers and haunts me constantly. I feel like that small, hateful, shitty man doing such harm to his own life. Enough with that now! I want to grow up now. But in what way? I am mature in many crucial ways. I just need to stop being afraid of upcoming life events and days. Normal damn days. I need to accept rather than to reject. I need to accept failure and move on. Give up about the past; the demons. Let it all go. Let it all be still. Still again as it was when I was a baby. At peace. That sounds strange; "As it was when I was a baby." But really, wouldn't it be nice. Being at peace. But then again, babies cry.

I want to be at peace. I want to be still but flowing at the same time. I am lazy and am such a failure in life. I don't work right now or go to school anymore. I tried both and, well, slipped away. I spend most my days trapped in an agonizing, mentally straining life style which takes up all my time, energy, purpose, and drive. It screws me over constantly; this "obsessive-compulsive disorder;" this mental and spiritual hell. This frustration. I want out…at the same time I need in. It sucks me in with such a powerful and heavy force. And then I feel guilty that I am complaining about my condition. I feel one-hundred percent responsible for my stupid insanity. Waahhh! Then I cry like a baby. It drives me out of my mind! But now I am going to play a different ballgame!

Attached to all my "issues" lie bad isolation and loneliness. It obviously comes with the territory. I am so used to being alone in my head. I am so adjusted to hiding out alone both mentally and physically. I need to use some sort of miraculous force to save my life and my situation. I need something more than myself. I need to tap into a different life force. I need a new energy. I wish for a new spirit; but in this life.

I do not want to die. I want to live a new, better, different life but at the same time remain alive in this life given to me by God. I want this life given to me and set up by me, but I wish for it to be healed. Healed either by myself or by God. I want to heal and live amazingly. I want satisfaction. I want peace in my journey. Is it a miracle that will save me? Will the supernatural work to heal my life? Or will it be the natural?

Is it even in my cards to be better? To be alive without worry or heartache. I feel I am suffering but I do not know true suffering. I feel I am suffering but that I bring it upon myself always. Is my karma that bad? Am I this pathetic? Have I always been this pathetic?

Waahhh! I cry! I cry all the time about this! I cry on the inside. My soul and spirit cry constantly! I whine to myself relentlessly. My damn internal dialogue.

My mind is like a machine which is always on; putting me in pain. In misery. Damn myself! I blame myself!

1-13-09

I pray to God. I pray for my family, myself, and all that I love. I want God in me at all times. I feel alone and useless. With God's help I will live free. What more can any man ask for but then to be with God? For a better life. Without God, one can feel ashamed.

A man woke up today ready to create life. He was ready to enter in. Get on into this game. Feels he's entered on into a new era of life. Somethings changed. There is a fire inside lit bright.

1-25-09

At least when I am writing my thoughts down on paper I am in control. I am choosing to take the time to finally express myself after holding my thoughts inside and holding my feelings on my face for so long. I have been treating myself poorly and I have been treating the people around me poorly. I have been taking loved ones for granted. I have been taking life for granted. I have been taking God for granted. Ease up boy. Ease up. Respect yourself. Enjoy it while alive. I am already twenty-five years old. A quarter of a century has gone by for me in this life. I have loved it. I have lived poorly through much of it, but in hind sight of course, I miss it. I think I should have lived better through it all, but I have had the opportunity to learn many lessons. I have enjoyed a lot of life as well. The learning process has the ability to be very exciting. I have been looking at my learning process into becoming a better man as very stressful and negative. That may be the problem after all. I am staring at my life trying to always change myself. Maybe I should just be myself and enjoy it. I should not take my life for granted any longer. I love my family so much. I love my parents so much. This is my nature. I do not always show it enough. I want to. I think a lot about being better. I would like to be better. Stronger mentally and spiritually; emotionally and physically. Underneath it all, I love this life of mine. I want to remain in it. This life of mine is perfect. Just as it is meant to be. I feel like I am a better person as I write my feelings down because I allow myself to focus only on my thoughts and feelings. Feelings are caused by thoughts. Thoughts are caused by feelings. When I clearly think I figure myself out. I get to the bottom of myself. I allow myself the chance to figure out what needs to be fixed. I am safe as long as I don't get stuck in my head. When I am trapped thinking, "forget about it." I get all messed up. I need to end that once and for all. Seems impossible really. I have become too paranoid. At first I believed it to be for my own good, but now it simply stresses me out to an insane degree. I must remedy this issue now. I am very unsuccessful by today's modern standard and it is eating me up inside. Poisoning my soul. I feel it and hate it. My worries are pathetic.

The only way to beat my obsessive-compulsive disorder is to live spiritually. I mean that I should live completely spiritually. Holy. I must live life holy. Naturally life is full of holiness. My obsessive-compulsive disorder causes me to be less aware and sensitive to life's holiness. The more I give into obsessive-compulsive disorder the less spiritual, holy, and lovely life is. The less spiritual, holy, and lovely I am as well. I hate standing by and watching this demon eat my life away. I accept this as if I cannot do anything to dissipate the pain of this hated life of mine. There is a side of life I dread. All my time here on Earth I fear it. I avoid waking from sleep so that I do not have to be a slave to this demon. I fear sleeping as well. I see it as only rest from a continuous force of bad energy. I sleep fearing and knowing that the OCD will be worse when I wake. I live this doomed cycle always. It must break. Now and forever. This is what I wish for. However, maybe I need to accept for less. I need to do as best I can with the time I have now and just accept that for what it is. Then as I live better my future will become more alive. Then as I live better my life now in the present moment will be more alive. Full of positive life is what I want to be. This is what I wish for. This is what I will be.

I am writing a prayer to God. For my family to be beautifully taken care of by you and for me to live a more beautiful life. Thank you God for this life of mine. Thank you God for the time I have had and for the time I do have. I love you God and worship you always.

Every day, twenty-four hours a day, I am living as a slave to obsessive-compulsive disorder. I am always susceptible to it and attached to what ever mental or physical chore it has assigned to me. Many times these chores are unrelated to one another. Once I have suffered through one ritual or chore, or whatever the hell I call it, there is another demon lurking ahead. There is always another task to get done. Anything that the OCD demands I comply with. I have to wash something or avoid something or mentally dissect an incident, event, or thought which occurred. A lot of thinking. Way too much thinking. All negative. All of these horrible OCD related tasks are so miserable. They are painful. They take their toll on me. They consume all of my energy. All of my energy is devoted to these ridiculously patterned acts of misery. I HATE this part of my life yet I do not change it. I try to but obviously not hard enough. The suffering will not end. The giving into and acceptance of my OCD is spiritually painful, emotionally painful, mentally painful, and even physically painful. This negative life cycle is killing me.

7-9-09

This past April I suffered a complete psychological breakdown. It has been a long time since I have written. I cannot fully describe to justice the hell that has attacked my life. My life has been stolen away completely and I am in a full out war to get it back. I am fighting every day as hard as my mind, body, and soul will let me. However the pain is immense. During the April psychological crash, the pain put me in unimaginable agony. I am a bit better. I have recovered a little but I am still suffering big-time. I have a long, hard journey ahead of me if I wish to kill my demon. Damn! What a turn for the worst. What has happened to me this past spring should happen to no one. Never in my life have I prayed so strongly that God is real. If so, I am comforted by the chance that this was not all random but maybe miraculously this is all happening for a reason.

My family took me in when my soul was dead. I was a barely living, barely breathing carcass of a man. I had been completely bed-ridden. I could not move. My older brother had to force me to eat bites of food. I became as pathetic and as dependant as a man can become. I still feel humiliated and ashamed by this experience. It was all so recent. I am in recovery now, but I am haunted by what has happened to me: a full out psychological breakdown. I lost my mind. I lost my life. I am doing what I can to recover what I have lost, but I am sad and depressed because I am nowhere near where I need to be. This is frightening. My life is dangling by a thread. The thread is being held by me; a man who suffers from serious, intense mental illness. I am sick. I do require medication. My life is torn but I am not giving up anymore. Before I had given up. Now I am fighting. The struggle I am facing now is one in which I need to fight to remain balanced psychologically, mentally, emotionally, and physically. This struggle is day to day. Literally hour to hour. Minute to minute. I hate this aspect of it. My life has become so temporary and incomplete. I want more positive permanence and well being. I need to feel complete again. Whole. I must be patient and remain to be a Soul Warrior.

What more can I do? Is it in my control? Is my life relying on the healing aspect of time? I am not sure but I am holding on for dear life and it hurts so badly. My pain is immense. The depression is looming over my head and body like a ghost. The sadness is extraordinary. The OCD is sickening. I have come to terms regarding how sick I truly am. It is healthy to realize one's own weakness. I must accept my mental disease to become stronger. Ironic 'aint it? It saddens me deeply but at the same time motivates me to heal and to become better. But I am so lonely. I am so alone. I feel so alone….I love my family more than life itself obviously. They are my reason for breathing, however, because of my battle with mental illness, I feel so alone.

One of the most important reasons I wish to heal is beside me. It is for my family. They have seen their son fallen. Now I wish for them to see their new son rise. I want to live well with my family for eternity. At my core, this is what matters to me. I pray to God. I thank God.

7-14-09

I cannot explain in words how hard it is to fight and fight second to second and to stay positive and hopeful. Never surrender! Never give up! This is some real hard shit to deal with. Especially because I blame myself and regret all of my choices. I am so mad at myself. I am living in regret of the past. I am living in fear of the future. Right now, in this moment, I feel pain.

Mental illness is extremely scary. I feel I am all by myself; sharing a body with a demon. Can you imagine being trapped inside a body with a demon who wants to eat you up; destroy you; kill your life? It is hell. I cannot bear to write of it anymore. The devil. Satan. Inside me. Around me. I pray for peace instead. I pray to God.

I have lost so much time. I have lost so much. Ruined so much. It is gone forever. Ruined forever...but so what. I HAVE WHAT IS LEFT!

It attacks me from all angles so often. I cannot take it. I try to sit still but cannot because my OCD is driving me crazy. It is driving me insane. I need more. I need my life to be better. I am searching for that everlasting, inner-loving peace. I will not try to search too hard or too gentle. I want the peace to last. I want to fight the darkness. I want to fight the loneliness. I want to fight the suffering.

7-15-09

My OCD is out of control. I am praying to be in control of my life. I want to be placed back on top of things but I fear that it is all too late. I am doomed. I need a way out of this mess I have created for myself. I am in pain and I am also tired. It is amazing. As I read back to last January, I realize just how much stronger, positive, and optimistic I was. I was hopeful. Or at least it seems that way now. That was all before the April crash. Realizing this is emotionally crushing. I have lost so much that I cannot even breathe anymore. I used to love life so much. I had a strong passion for living and now I have nothing. I know underneath that I love life, I just cannot feel it. I wish to feel this passion for life once again.

This pain I feel is unbearable. I wish that God would give me the right words to express myself. I wish that God would give me the right prayers to heal. I need help. I need mercy.

I choose to write about my pain and frustration in hopes that it will benefit my mental health. I want to put my feelings onto paper to heal myself. My depression aches my whole body, my whole mind, my whole soul. I am destroyed from within and it is crushing my outside world. Any way to feel better I will take. Any measure to heal is the path which I shall walk. I pray for another chance at life. A good life. I have so much yet I am blind to truly see any of it. I am not physically starving as so many in this world are yet I find reason to complain because my mental health is malnourished. My soul is literally starving for something else; something more. God help me. Protect my family. Let us all live in bliss. I pray for harmony. For belonging. I wish for an end to my longing for something more. I wish to be satisfied with what I already have in front of me. I contradict myself: I want more yet at the same time I pray to be satisfied with what I already do have.

10-13-09

I see now how hopeless my situation is. I am doomed. I live in a little shit-shack of loneliness and depression. I do love that my apartment has heat in the winter. It could be worse. I could have no heat in the winter. I see this one positive point, but it is so much worse than that. I feel suicidal. I know, cliché, right. But I feel so worthless and alone. I feel down right miserable. I could not kill myself for one important reason: my family. To put them through the death of a loved one would be the ultimate sin. How selfish it would be. But my lows are so low. I feel that other than my family, which whom I love so very much, I've got nothing. I am currently living on social security for my mental disability. I have been living on social security since I was eighteen years old. I am ashamed by this but I know that I need this aid desperately so that I can get by. I need it to survive. I am so sick right now. I can barely take care of myself. I am in fact ashamed and embarrassed by my life situation. It is pathetic. I am so full of self-hatred and self-loathing. It consumes me and drives me crazy. I wouldn't take my own life but it runs through my mind. Suicide. I hate the idea. Get out of me sickness! I hate you for ruining my whole, entire life!

I promise that I will not act on this harassing, sickening feeling. Suicide. How very miserable the idea feels to me. But it is my feeling; a feeling which is my right. It is my right to feel so bad but I do not choose it. It hurts so bad. I want to live and live well of course. I wish that I could enjoy every or any moment, no matter how significant or insignificant. I must learn that if I am unable to enjoy every moment I should at least try to enjoy some. I am tired of shying away from simple pleasures because I am ashamed of myself. How sad.

I am feeling so sad and alone. Completely empty. My life will never get better. I am only going down. I wish that God would allow me to come up with the right words to make my life better. I would write them. Praying is all I have. I write to you God. My writing is my prayer. I pray to you on paper and in my head. Please be real. Please do not abandon me. Fill my body with life. Good life. I need it now more than ever. I wish to enjoy what life I have left. I am twenty-six years old. I can live on. Please God, give me the strength and willpower to move on.

I pray for a beautiful life. I know I must seem needy, but my sight lacks beauty. I do not see beauty in my life. I am nervous. So nervous. My nerves have gotten the best of me and are forcing me way down hill. If I had permanent beauty in my life I would be a satisfied man. I pray for permanent beauty God. I pray for a piece of the miracle which is life.

11-18-09

It is so frustrating. What I want to do more than anything is write but my OCD has me terrified of the ink which writes my words. OCD causes irrational fears that would not bother most functional people. Right now I am terrified that if I get ink on my hand I will have to spend an extended amount of time exerting all of my energy washing it off. Boy I do a lot of washing. I cannot afford a laptop right now, so that is not a solution.

I woke up so late today. Around 7:00 P.M. ... I was too depressed to face the day. To face reality. I actually had a very important errand to run. I was supposed to go down to my old school, a small community college in Wellesley, Massachusetts, and withdraw from a class. If I fail to do this tomorrow I flunk the class and my GPA will go way down. My anxiety about this whole situation is burdening me like fire. So instead of completing my one responsibility, I rationalized that staying in bed was the better option. I pretended that I was dead to the world.

Oh I feel so horrible. I feel so talent-less. I do feel dead to the world. I can tell how sick I am right now based purely on my bad penmanship. My penmanship is also bad because as I write, I am doing my best to avoid the ink from the pen. OCD, what a horror. It must seem so easy to combat if you do not have OCD, but if you do, my God! I wish that I had something more interesting to tell you right now but I am so scared that I cannot think straight.

12-3-09

I am so desperately lonely right now. Nothing can comfort or cure me but everything frightens me in this world of OCD. I want so bad to be like the normals; able to function in society. Still, I understand that others have their own pain, but mine is what I know and all I can feel.

I am sick with anticipation of what will go wrong next. What hell will I create for myself? I pray for joy. I pray for peace. What if I amount to nothing because of my condition? I am terrified of this. My God, I am on four different medications for my poor mental health. Is this what God intended for me when I was created? I want more for myself because one day I WILL DIE. I want more for myself so that I can show my family that their beloved son is alive. The written word has power. Maybe my words will heal me. Maybe they will help heal another human being. Then I have accomplished. Then I have succeeded.

However, this seems so far off. What other human is interested in my nonsense of a life? Am I writing a book or is this therapy? Perhaps both. That is my dream: that my written word will change me or if not me then some other soul.

Day after day I go through this same system of OCD and depression. It is killing my sleep cycle. I am tired yet cannot sleep; I am awake but only want to sleep. It confuses me too. Where do I go from here? God help me.

I whine, yes, but this is my right as a human being. To question. To demand more. This is my right and I will use it as a tool to heal in some way. If it takes all of my life, so be it. I must try. I need to challenge myself. I need to move with life even though it feels as if life is moving against me. What do I do? I must continue to fight.

12-6-09

I am so angry right now. Everything was fine. Or so in my mind it seems as though things were fine compared to right now. I came home after a pleasant evening with family and immediately the rituals began. The loss of control attacked me like a ton of bricks. When you are swept away by the OCD, it is nearly impossible to set yourself free. I became stuck doing physical rituals, opposed to mental rituals, to humiliating to write down onto paper. Beside the humiliation is the pain. I feel it now. The regret of what could have been had I not begun with the rituals in the first place. I feel that the grass is always greener wherever I am not. The rituals of my OCD hurt my soul, mind, and body. They cause major depression and suicidal thinking (in extreme cases). The levels of OCD vary, but in my case it is no light matter. This is a heavy burden I despise carrying. As I write I feel like crying. I wish that I had something better to write about, but this is my sad reality.

I want to write so that someone else who needs the help I do can relate to my words. Also, the writing helps me feel better about myself. It feels somewhat productive and when I write I am not giving into obsessive-compulsive disorder. Writing definitely helps with my depression. I am putting some of my pain onto paper. Maybe that pain can somehow disappear forever.

I may write scattered thoughts, but I am not trying to be a guru or the next Socrates. I am a man in pain who is looking for an outlet and at the same time is trying to help others who are suffering. Those who feel helpless as I do now. How can I help myself? I am so terrified that I will amount to nothing. I fear what the future holds for me. I am writing to help myself; to free my soul. I want others who struggle to read my words. But then I ask myself again, "why would anyone want to read my words?"

I feel so terrible about giving into my OCD; so beaten down. Like a true failure. I want to go back in time and try to save myself before the crash last April. I want to be my own hero, but that would be impossible because I already played the role of being my own worst enemy. I need a miracle to battle this demon. This is a real chemical imbalance inside my brain. My disability is physical, not only mental, and I cannot stop it from destroying my life. God help me.

I pray to be my own hero!

12-11-09

It is tragically comedic how bad I am suffering over something most people would not be frightened by. It all began yesterday afternoon when I received a call from a friend to come over and relax while he was doing his laundry. At the time it seemed like a good idea. I did not have anything to do anyway. However the shit was going to hit the fan very soon and I was not prepared. OCD is a trickster in all forms. Why did I not realize that if another human is doing laundry; handling filthy, used clothing and underwear; that they are in my definition automatically intensely contaminated? What a fool I am.

As I watched my friend do his laundry and handle a load of dirty clothing it all hit me. CONTAMINATION! My heart began to pound and my anxiety skyrocketed to an eleven out of ten. I then knew that I was doomed. I knew that my friend's hands were contaminated. I was hoping he would wash them but like a care-free, normal, functioning human he did not. I wanted so badly to request that my friend wash his hands but I could not bring myself to request that of him. Maybe it was out of shame, guilt, or humiliation. Really it was all three. Then all hell broke loose. This friend happens to be of an affectionate nature. He is rather physical. With his contaminated hands he grabbed me in a playful manner. My world stopped. I was sick with anxiety. I could not believe the hell that I had walked right into. He kept touching me. My coat, my pants. Now all ruined. All contaminated. I should have simply asked him to wash his hands after handling his dirty cloths. "If only. If only I had not done this. If only I had done that instead." It is always "if only" some other outcome had occurred. Then I would be fine. But I am not fine at all.

Today the OCD is weighing heavy on my shoulders. The feeling of being contaminated is killing my soul. I feel that contaminated cells are all over my coat and pants. I purposely wore the same pants today in an attempt to conquer this demon, but I only feel like 'contaminated shit.' I like that term. But I did it all to myself. How could I have not realized that going to a house where another human is handling their dirty clothing is bound to be a huge mistake? Now I am stuck being contaminated. I can wash everything which had been touched, but that would only be giving into the OCD. To battle OCD one must deal with the anxiety and not respond to it. Sit with it. This is what I have learned, but it hurts so badly. What can I do? I cannot live like this. I still feel sick about it the next day. When will the sickness die?

I am literally shaking right now stewing in the contamination. A person suffering with OCD may think about microscopic cells, unseen to the naked eye. This person knows that these microscopic cells do exist; whether or not they can be seen. Unless they are washed away they will never go away. They will remain. They will not die. Illogical as it may seem, this is my condition. I did not sign up for this and I hate it, but I give into it. I am trying to fight. I am trying to ignore. I am trying to move on without washing my contaminated articles of clothing, but it is just so anxiety provoking. That is an understatement. There is a sense of doom which now exists in my life which was not there before I walked into my friend's house yesterday. It is important to note that my friend is not at all responsible for my pain now. It is my own entire fault. I should have known the misery which was about to occur. I cannot escape this OCD. I cannot escape these contaminated cells because they are everywhere.

How much more of this hell can I take? My whole life has been derailed because of OCD. I really do not see an escape or a solution. Writing is my best therapy. It allows my worries to be seen on paper and not only lived through in my own existence. My consciousness feels faded away into nothingness.

Back to the laundry story. I feel so guilty about writing it onto paper now. I do not want my good, innocent friend to feel bad in anyway. I am the sick one. I know he will read this one day so I pray that he understands that it is my own fault and no blame goes to him. He is a great guy and not a dirty person. Maybe this has all been a blessing in disguise to strengthen me. Then I owe that friend a thank you. It is just the OCD. It is not me. My brother tells me that instead of getting mad by the many triggers of my OCD and the many events that occur which escalate my OCD, I should instead get mad that I care at all about this bullshit. In other words, instead of worrying and becoming angry about my precious bubble being popped I should only be angry that I have a precious bubble in the first place. No human should be forced to live trapped in a bubble. I should be angry that I have no true freedom because of my mental condition. I desire mental and spiritual freedom and if this requires living in contamination I should take the deal. How grand life would be if I had none of these irrational fears and issues. How grand life can be.

I dream that this book, this story, be published one day and that others read it. I know that there are others suffering as well. Maybe quietly, maybe out loud, but they are alive and if they can relate to my story, than we are sharing the burden and some of the weight is lessened for each of us.

1-11-10

Just to be alive I have so much, but I cannot help to feel so much pain as well. The most insignificant tasks or annoyances bother me to such an insane degree. Day to day living leaves me a torn, conflicted human being. There is so much emotional and mental strain in my life. However, because I have been working hard to live a better more positive existence I occasionally get very brief moments of satisfaction. Very brief and very sporadic. I often find myself terrified by the upcoming moments of my life. I become paralyzed because I have such intense OCD and depression. As a matter of fact, it bothers me to refer to my condition as obsessive-compulsive disorder. It sounds too clinical. There is more hell to my condition; a negative feeling that is more morbid than the title "OCD" can express. I do want out of this mess and I am trying desperately to find ways to heal or escape the misery. You see, that is the attitude I need. I need to work my hardest to stay positive and strong through the worst of times. It takes mental, emotional, and spiritual toughness. I need to believe in something other than only pain in my life. I need joy. I need joy so that I can bring joy to others, especially my family whom I love the most out of all aspects of life. Spending time, caring for, and enjoying time with my family are the most important choices in my life. To make these proper choices one needs to have joy. I love my friends as well. To share joy with them is a path I wish to walk. God I wish to have joy. I wish to share joy with my family. I wish to share joy with my friends. When I am alone I feel the most pain. I also wish that this painful loneliness disappears and is replaced with lonesome joy instead.

1-27-10

I still feel such a strong sense of purposelessness. I am not doing well. My luck with exposure therapy is taking its toll on me. I find myself pacing from room to room with nothing to do but to mourn the passing moments of my passing youth. I get little satisfaction and I am poor financially. They say money is the root of all evil. Maybe, but I could sure use some to increase the quality of my life. I do not know what to do with myself. First of all I am dependent on medication. Fine, I am sick. This was God's plan all along (I hope). But now I am beginning to rely on sleeping aids because my sleep cycle is so messed up and inconsistent. I need to stop. Addiction to sleeping aids is very unhealthy. I want to wake up earlier in the day but I am too discouraged during that lonely period of waking. The loneliest time is trying to fall asleep. Racing thoughts, anxiety, and sadness. All of it is so intense. I do like being asleep however. The ultimate escape. But then I awake. Bam! Back to reality. A reality which I find hard to bear. What do I do God? How do I change this? I need purpose. I need something more than mental illness. I should volunteer somewhere and help others, but that is so hard for a human being such as me to do. To be on a fixed schedule right now seems impossible. I am in debt because in an attempt to escape pain, I have been going out with friends and I have been spending all my cash on booze. It feels good but it is so bad for me psychologically, physically, and financially. I crave booze right now as I write. What a life! God, I am looking for a good change. Please help me find it. Thank you.

2-1-10

Up until this point in my writing my OCD has hindered my ability to bring my writing journal outside of my apartment. Unfortunately this is a common symptom of the disease. Well, today for the first time I decided that I would write in public at the local coffee shop. This is quite significant for my recovery. This is a big challenge. I am obviously worried that my journal will become contaminated and as a result all my writing will be gone to waste. But I must combat these feelings. This is a goal of mine; to combat all of these obsessive fears. It is time I become the **SOUL WARRIOR** I was born to be. It will take strength and pain of course. It will take courage. This is a mental disease we are talking about. Irrational as it may seem, it is real. *You are what you believe.* I can let the OCD beat me or I can beat the OCD. Is my mind ready? Is my soul ready?

On top of the OCD lies the depression. The failure. I hate myself for this. So far in life I have been very hard on myself because I have been unable to achieve success. I see all the productive, successful members of society, right here in this coffee shop, and it forces me to feel miserable. Is the OCD what has caused my failure? Or is it that I lack a certain ambition that the successful people do have? Obviously my OCD hinders my ability to become successful, but I still choose to desire success.

I feel sad and guilty because I feel that I am a failure. Sometimes walking through the streets can be very painful. The comparisons I make. I feel beneath. This is unhealthy. I recognize this fact. How can I feel on top if I do not have the job or the proper education that is so desired and necessary to be considered successful? What can a mentally ill man offer to society? I need to get my shit organized.

Why can't I look out the window of this coffee shop and watch life, watch the world, watch the sky and feel successful? Why do I feel the need to prove myself? To compare. I am my own man. My own self. I am dealing with my own complicated issues. I need to loosen up on myself. I need to erase my opinion of myself. Erase my ego. I must learn from life, not loath it. Enough pain. Enough suffering. Is it in my own power? Is it in God's power? Or both?

I become so desperate that in fact I find myself leaning and depending upon God for help. I then feel guilt for asking too much of this idea of God. I feel shame for relying on God. What if God cannot help my situation and it simply is not in my cards to heal? But I want to believe in God. I want to depend on God. The idea of God gives me comfort. The idea of God gives me hope and puts me at ease. I choose to worship God not to gain but because it feels right to do so. I want more out of my life, which can be considered gain, but I cannot help myself from asking God to allow me to attain more out of life. Is this asking for too much gain or is it my birthright to ask this of God?

My pain feels immeasurable and incurable, but I will triumph. I want this to be my new life. I want this change. I cannot write of this anymore today. I must now live it. I must move with God or the power that be which I feel and am aware of. I must now put this method of living into practice. I must walk this path. The path of a soul warrior. I want to believe.

2-9-10

After all my optimism of becoming a soul warrior, I once again have let the shit hit the fan. I feel low again. I have let my drinking habit take a turn for the worse. I became blackout drunk during the Super Bowl and regret it sincerely. I am too reliant on drugs. Because of this my stress and depression have worsened. My financial state is in crisis. I have done this all to myself and I am angry.

I am so worried about becoming broke again. My lovely and caring older brother had to give me $330 to save my ass. I am nervous I will get into another financial mess. I am worried. Financial stability is crucial in regards to a sense of security in today's society. Being broke leaves one feeling weak, alone, and vulnerable. I hate the idea of money but it affects even I who claims to be a soul warrior.

2-16-10

How can I change my negative outlook on life? Negativity consumes my existence, but I believe that this can all change. I cannot tolerate the bad any longer so I must fight to make my life of a higher quality. I can pray, meditate, continue with the medication, and continue to explore spirituality; all of the above. But what counts is that I stick to it. I will be able to re-train my brain and alter my consciousness for the better.

I have been abusing alcohol recently but I am trying to quit. When I drink it is obviously to escape. I cannot escape from life anymore. The harder it gets the more involved I need to be in improving my situation. Out of any obstacle there is an opportunity for a solution. Out of any problem there is an opportunity to heal.

My body works and I am grateful for this. It is my brain, or mind, which is malfunctioning. But if a human can change their body with hard work, than certainly a human can also change their brain, or mind, with committed and hard work. It can be done. My mind can heal. My life can improve. Suddenly I feel more optimistic!

I fear the reader may find my thoughts uninteresting or insignificant, however before passing judgment one must comprehend that this dream I have of healing mentally and spiritually is all I have. It is all I have to aspire to. A person afflicted with mental illness wants only one thing: to get better mentally. You see, I am not fascinated by cars, computers, technology, or fashion. I am not interested in attaining the highest degree or nailing the best job. These materialistic ideas and fancy positions are unimportant to me in my life. All that fascinates me is the idea, or rather the dream, that maybe I can beat my mental disease. This is what I want. It is what I need. I dream of balance between my mind, body, and soul. I will not quit until I achieve this goal.

2-20-10

It is all like a roller coaster ride with this OCD. Walking down the street is terrifying. I do not know who I will see or whose hand I will have to shake. Very recently I ran into an old friend. In my head I was very worried and preoccupied with contamination. After shaking hands with this friend my world was turned upside down. I had only one option. Run into the local frozen yogurt store with a public restroom and wash my hands compulsively and furiously. Not very fun considering the fact that I loathe using public restrooms. Quite embarrassing and painful indeed.

I avoid waking up from sleep. Today I rose at 4:30 P.M. I lied in bed for hours tragically avoiding life. I do this because I know what I must do when I wake. I must get ready for the day which requires a very vigorous obsessive-compulsive shower. It is torture for the soul.

I do not know what else to say. Because of my mental illness I am avoiding life and missing all of its beauty. Where do I go from here? One day I am motivated and ready to change my life for the better but on other days I enter the repetitive cycle of OCD and depression. Hopelessness. I am consumed with worry about the future to a degree where I am unable to enjoy the present moment. What I need to grasp is that there is no future. It is only a concept in my mind. All I have is right now. I must admit that I am dissatisfied with right now but obsessing about tomorrow and the days which follow only puts more weight on my back. Positive one day. Negative the next. Positive one hour. Negative the next. This is the *suffer cycle*. I dream of disconnecting from this nightmare. I hate it.

I wish that I could use my mind to create a breakthrough. An epiphany. I want to heal so badly and feel better. I dream of this, so why does it not come true. I assume my mental illness is so hard to combat because of its biological roots in my DNA. Mental illness is genetic after all, and it does run in my family. So what do I do? How can I overcome genetics? Seems impossible. Is it? The only entity or idea I can think of to allow or help me to heal is what I call "God." When a man must combat a seemingly insurmountable genetic affliction the only option to winning is turning to a higher power. A power beyond comprehension. I need God to allow me to heal. What other choice do I have? Mental illness is both biological and environmental. I am working hard to alter my environment for the better, but how can I change my biological make-up? Seems impossible really. But when life's problems seem impossible to destroy, how can one not turn to a higher power? My options are limited. I can either choose to rot away or to fight and believe in this incomprehensible higher power. Whatever this power may be. May it be God? May it be outside of me? May it be inside of me? Does God owe me anything as my birthright? Is this blasphemy to ask such a question? Do I owe something to God? I believe I do. I believe I owe all my being to God. Is this my proof? Is this my proof that God, this higher power, is all I have to turn to? Is this my proof that God is real? I feel this power. I desire to be a part of this *God-frequency*. When I suffer I do pray to feel better. Do I deserve to change from being suicidal to believing in God? Relying on God?

I realize that these questions have been asked throughout all the ages of mankind, but it is new to me. I have been distracted my whole life. Distracted by my mental afflictions. I am not special because I am asking these deep questions. I am as equal to any other human. But I am special because I now believe that I am a child of God. No matter what age you are, we are all children of God. We are all special. This higher power must exist. I certainly am banking on this. Without a higher power to turn towards, I will be unable to rise above my biological illness and disability. Yes, mental illness is a disability.

2-24-10

I am ready for something new. Something different. I want to live my life closer to God. Closer to my family. This is a path to the bliss I desire. For anyone reading this that is in pain, or for a reader's loved one that is in pain, you must never give up the battles. Loosing is a part of this war for a better life. I still remember the days of life where I would stare at the blades of kitchen knives and imagine cutting into my throat. Those days are over but it took hard, grueling emotional and spiritual work to end them. From suicide to God. This is where I have come. I feel a sense of well being. I am trying to stay present in the moment. I am tired of being haunted by the past and terrified of the future. Enough is enough. 'PMA.' Present Moment Awareness is my new tool to living in the now and avoiding the suffering and anxiety that the past and future hold for me. Remember, the past and future do not exist. There is only now. I know the pain of wanting to die. I understand it and will never forget it. But now I am equipped with a new feeling. The will to live. The will to survive. This is true empowerment. True courage. Everyone has access to it. Even the mentally ill. The mentally ill or the mentally unfortunate can become the mentally sound and the mentally fortunate. It is hard work but it can be done. Stay in the now and time will pass; time will heal. Your pain can blossom into your greatest strength. Overcoming life's obstacles will turn you into your own hero. It will put you in the position of the conqueror-not the conquered. This mentality must be engrained in your mind time and time again until it sticks. If it does not stick, try again. What other choice do we have? Life is meant to be hard so that the reward from God can be great. The reward can be attainable only if we see each obstacle as an opportunity. Do not kill yourself. There is always another chance. Another way. That chance may take the form as another obstacle which causes great pain, but with a new perspective, this new obstacle maybe the opportunity of a lifetime.

2-25-10

I failed miserably last night. I had an OCD attack, even after writing all about change and staying positive. But life is different now. I will embrace this familiar suffering. I will not let it bother me. Yes, my anxiety over last night's obsessive-compulsive situation is high, but I am using this anxiety to strengthen my mind and soul. How? I am simply sitting with it. I am embracing it. Accepting it as fate. I made a mistake last night, but in life humans are meant to make mistakes so that they can grow. We can grow by learning from the experience and we can grow by enduring the pain that the experience brings.

My whole view on pain and suffering has changed. I will embrace the pain. I will accept the suffering. This is my opportunity to rise above and overcome. This is my moment. My moment to excel in life. To survive with all the pain vibrating and radiating throughout all the cells in my body. My body will endure. My mind will endure. This is the path to freedom. It is my birth-right to endure pain and to survive.

It is my birth-right to live free.

2-27-10

I am trying to write to heal myself and at the same time I am trying to help other human beings who struggle as I do. This cycle of OCD and depression is taking its toll on me severely. However, I will not quit in my attempt to reclaim my life. I will survive the pain, major depression, and anxiety. I will not take my own life. I will live in this life and do what I can to improve my situation. But attempting to constantly improve my own life situation has its downside. It allows me to believe that what I have right here in front of me, 'my life in the present,' is not good enough. This alone is very discouraging. Maybe the key is not to constantly improve my situation but instead, I should simply accept what is right before my eyes. Constantly attempting to improve and being unaccepting of the 'now' forces one to be obsessed with a better future. I do not believe that this is the best option I have. Instead, maybe I should put my energy on right now and accept it. Again, focusing only on the future is focusing on an idea that is not real. It will never be the future; it will always be right now. I must accept now for what it is worth, even if accepting the now is accepting pain. Taking the pain of the present moment will toughen up the mind and soul. I can concentrate on how bad right now really is, but eventually I will be desensitized to the pain. If I keep focusing on how bad right now is, and simply sit with the pain, anxiety, depression, and frustration, eventually my mind will become desensitized to all the negativity. Time will pass. I will remain in the present moment, and maybe, just maybe, I will heal by accepting the hell of mental illness. I will become accustomed to the hell and the hell will dissipate. By accepting the painful present moment,

I will become accustomed to this constant string of the now, and with extreme patience, the now and 'the acceptance of the now' will be easier to live in. The truth is that this mind and soul exercise is extremely tough and painful, but it maybe my only hope to joy and to the wonderful acceptance of the 'now' which is called life.

2-28-10

It is unfair to a strong degree. I have figured out that obstacles are opportunities for great change and growth but after learning this, it seems that the obstacles are growing stronger. My life situation has worsened in the past few days, but now I realize that it could be for an ironic reason. Through my pain comes the growth. I know this but I was naive. I figured out a key to the lock of life; that pain is the path to freedom. But since figuring this out the pain has only increased. This, I did not expect. What can I do? I have learned to sit with the pain of the present moment so that I can become desensitized to the pain. Sticking to this plan however is the hard part. Right now in the present moment I am being greatly challenged with irrational, obsessive-compulsive ideas. They are driving me into being extremely unhappy and uncomfortable. Can this discomfort really serve me by leading me into a positive direction? Why does it hurt so bad to grow stronger? I think I have the answer. If I were to aspire to strengthen my physical body, I would have to put my body through the intense pain of working out. Well the brain is a physical entity that can change as well. I am supposed to exercise the mind to strengthen it. Instead of a total body workout, I am putting my mind through a total brain workout. This is why the pain is so intense today. I am working out my mind by looking at my life obstacles as opportunities. Yes, this is hard to do but this is the workout my mind needs. This is how I will strengthen my brain. If I can't cure my mental disease I will do everything in my power to beat it.

3-4-10

Life begins from here. I am still struggling with my OCD and cannot seem to shake the depression. When I do have brief moments of contentment, which I do appreciate and am grateful for, I then begin to worry about how long the fulfillment will last. Once the worry begins, the fulfillment ends and I am stuck on the other side of contentment. I need to figure out a way to let go of the worry and simply accept these rare, fulfilling, positive moments when I have them without any conception of how long they will last. Again, this is a negative trait. It is a preoccupation with time which is bad. I feel good and then crush the positivity by worrying about the future. I wonder how I can, after so much pain and suffering, create lasting fulfillment and harmony; lasting joy. It seems out of reach. "It seems out of reach!" I need to end this negative internal dialogue. Negative self talk kills the psyche. Positive internal dialogue or positive thinking really is curing and soothing. My only problem is that most of the time I cannot overlook the distracting pain and fill my mind with positivity or light. I stay the same and keep the darkness in my mind and in my soul.

A great weapon to combat the darkness is simply the observance of the negativity. Watch the negativity. Wait for it to come. Expect it. Then when you witness the negativity by feeling the emotional pain it causes, at least you are in the present moment aware of the havoc the negative thinking is reaping upon your life and your soul. Simply being aware is the key to unlocking the magic. The beauty in life. When you are aware that there is no beauty in your life at the present moment you can then ask why. The answer will be 'perspective.' This negative outlook which steals your beauty away is your developed negative perspective on life which is stealing your life and energy away. But how can one simply change their whole perspective on life? After all, it has taken a lifetime to develop this negative perspective. To successfully change your perspective on your current life situation is extremely challenging and it may take all the time in the world to do so, but one who is suffering must try!

One idea to begin this journey of change is by changing ones internal dialogue from negative to positive. Instead of berating myself silently in my head for having mental problems and for not being a success, I must change my internal dialogue to one of compassion for my own self. Treat yourself kindly. True compassion. Aside from the weaknesses I have, I need to shift gears to find my strengths. Then once I realize my strengths I am allowed to praise myself internally. The point is not to be cocky or egotistical; it is to be compassionate. This praise is positive. Suddenly there is some positive internal dialogue running through your mind. Eventually this positive internal dialogue will touch your soul. Again if you suffer from mental illness and depression, as I do, switching gears from negative to positive can at times seem impossible, but this goal of saving one's own life is the greatest challenge one will ever face. This concept of impossibility is a symptom of the mental illness or depression. Going step by step is another key. Take it slowly. Life does not need to be rushed. Little bits of positivity entering your mind can add up and before you know it you are practicing positive thinking and the result is that you are now retraining your brain. This is challenging, but stay positive and this mission becomes a real, worthwhile possibility. One which will save your existence by trading away negativity and darkness for positivity and light. This is the greatest option one will ever have.

3-4-10

I find myself being so self conscious. I am constantly aware of how people might be seeing me. It is as if I am a slave to society. A slave to the approval of others. I pray that I defeat this self consciousness which weighs heavy on me and negatively affects my life. I always notice my mistakes and am constantly judging myself because of them. This is obviously a part of my mental illness. When I feel I have done something stupid or unbecoming in front of another I suffer so much regret and depression. I need to develop the strength to not care about the opinions of others. I need to be confident, but not overly confident because after all, it is human nature to make mistakes. When I do make these mistakes however, it is absolutely necessary that I do not judge myself and live in shame about an insignificant event that has already past. This is how I can grow from a mistake. By letting it go and not being affected by it negatively. Never be worried about how others judge you and do not judge your own self. Always have the strength to move on. Mistakes are always meant to be. They occur so that we may overcome them, thereby strengthening ourselves. Mistakes occur so that we are able to strengthen our own minds and our souls. We are then on a positive path.

3-5-10

It is clear to me now that I am prone to making mistakes and acting like a fool. I have been trying to stay away from drugs and alcohol for a while now. Last night I went out with my good friends with the intention of staying sober. But I screwed up. I gave into the temptation of instant gratification. I had partaken in doing drugs again and drinking alcohol, which is a drug as well. It felt great at the time. Pure instant gratification. But it took a toll on my psyche. I woke up today late in the afternoon feeling depressed and defeated. I had failed my goal of staying sober. I could feel the physical and mental weakness that the partying had caused. I was full of regret, but again humans are meant to make mistakes.

I now realize that giving into the instant gratification of drugs was all part of the plan. I needed to wake up this morning in regret so that the next time I am tempted, I will remember the feeling of the morning after. The feeling is unpleasant. The feeling is undesirable. But the feeling is in my control. I can avoid it. It's like a tradeoff: Get high with instant gratification one night but the next morning have no sense of well being. I need to remember this. Temptation is a bitch.

3-5-10

I desire a higher sense of well being. I am working to attain this. I crave it and will achieve it. What I am looking for is not instant gratification. What I am looking for is a *'new consciousness.'* One which includes lasting bliss and harmony. A sense of well being that does not flee away after each mistake I make. I want a sense of well being strong enough to never part from my psyche and my soul. I know that this may seem out of reach because I have been suffering from a mental disease since childhood, but why is it impossible? I have the power and the desire. I am a true soul warrior. As long as I do not quit then I can still succeed. I find it fascinating how much my sense of what success is has changed. I used to believe success to be material worth. Now I believe it to be spiritual, emotional, and psychological self worth. How freeing. I choose to live apart from the material and physical world of yesterday and instead choose to be a part of a new and better conciousness. A consciousness of today. A consciousness of the now. A consciousness strong enough not to flee away. A consciousness which is indestructible, immovable, and everlasting. I dream of a new, better, lovely consciousness; one which cannot be touched. I will not quit until this new consciousness is mine! It cannot be understated how important attaining this new consciousness is, but be prepared to fall. This is a growing process after all, and as discussed before, to grow one must make mistakes. One must fall and get back up bigger and stronger. I expect hard spots in the road, but I will not let them sidetrack me away from my dream. Deal with the bumps in the road and move on. All the bumps are meant to be experienced so that we can gain our new consciousness. It will not be handed to us. We must work hard to attain this gift of all gifts. This is our purpose!

3-6-10

Life throws curveballs my way and I find it frustrating. I would simply like to wake up and live my life according to plan. 'According to plan' is a way of life that allows me to enjoy every second with no interruption. Sadly, interruptions are an integral part of life. They come in the form of obstacles there to laugh in your face. I just experienced a severe obstacle and my OCD and anxiety level have increased severely. I don't know how to get through it. I wrote earlier that mistakes are meant to be and that obstacles are really opportunities, but this is painful. I am not sure if my hands are contaminated, and more intense is my doubt that this obstacle has happened for a specific reason. I guess it is to make me stronger, but guessing is not good enough. I need to know that it happened for a reason. It is killing me. Second guessing one's own action is extremely unhealthy, but I am doing it now. I need to stop.

3-7-10

Where do I go from here, or rather, where do I grow from here? I went through a hard struggle yesterday, but, of course survived. The aftershock of anxiety remains however I feel the obstacle has been overcome allowing me to grow a bit stronger. A bit mentally tougher. But the anxiety of yesterday is still radiating throughout my body. I need to shake it or better yet simply observe it and let it dissipate on its own.

I am still too self conscious. I was at a bar two nights ago with my brother and some great friends. We had a fantastic night. But then yesterday, some other friends wanted to go back to the same bar. I was strongly opposed. I did not want to relive an experience which already went so well. Unfortunately I gave in. This story is not meant to be deep or symbolic. The situation that occurred is made of pure vanity. I went to the bar where the same beautiful, female bartender was working. But I had on the same sweatshirt I had worn the night before. Because of this I feel that the bartender noticed and was judging the fact that I had the same sweatshirt on two nights in a row. How vain am I to care. Again, I admit this is not some deep or significant problem. It is simply proof of how self conscious I am and how much I am a slave to the judgment of others and of society. I feel better having written this experience down. No real growth has come from it, but still, it feels better knowing how silly my insecurities are. If only I did not have a crush on the local bartender. How typical.

What a trivial preoccupation I am having with this but if you could see how beautiful this bartender is, you would understand my insecurity. A girl that pretty is a girl I want to impress. I do not want her to have a negative opinion of me. What can I do? I sure 'aint going to the bar three nights in a row. Two nights seems pathetic enough. This is proof of how a little insecurity can sky rocket into something debilitating and huge.

I need to attain the ability to control my emotions. This is a skill humans have been trying to attain for thousands of years. I am realizing new things about myself and my interactions with others. But, I still am struggling with the feelings of regret and emptiness. These are obviously symptoms of depression. "Where do I go from here?" This is the question I keep asking myself. I need something more profound to be thinking of other than some girl's opinion of me. I want to move away from this side of life. I do not want to be trapped any longer with insecurity which leads to depression. I must toughen up now! If obstacles are meant to happen for a reason then this is all for a reason. I must not loose sight of this! Where do I grow from here?

The OCD does not help with my insecurity of seeming pathetic in front of a girl I find so beautiful. I keep *obsessively* thinking about our interaction last night opposed to the night before. These thinking patterns are *compulsive* as well. They are ruining my present moment which puts all this in the category of obsessive-compulsive disorder.

3-8-10

Today's events were excruciating. I have a very specific system of how I get ready in the time after arising from sleep, which usually takes the place of any random P.M. hour around the clock. I always routinely wash my hands before taking my medicine, however today I did not. It was an accident. My world became crushed. I felt that I had just contaminated all of my medicine bottles. I had contaminated each and every one. My anxiety rose to be off the scale. My day had been ruined along with the days following the contamination. Also, in my panic, I lost sight of the idea that mistakes are meant to be and that obstacles are really opportunities in disguise. All I cared about was my stupid mistake. All I could feel was anxiety and regret. The weather outside was beautiful for early March, but because of my mistake, I would not allow myself to feel the sun's glory. The soothing late winter air was blowing right by me but I would not let myself enjoy its mild warmth. I spent the next couple of hours suffering with anxiety but I knew that I was going to take matters into my own obsessive-compulsive hands. In a panic I threw all the contaminated medicine bottles away in the trash and put all the medicinal pills in clean paper cups. This relieved the anxiety. It seems crazy, but this is what it took to take all the anxiety away. Obviously I performed an obsessive-compulsive hand wash before handling the situation. This was not my favorite day of the season.

What hurts the most is that I was put to the test but I did not pass. I let my OCD get the best of me. I lost sight of the idea that mistakes are meant to occur and that this obstacle I was facing could have existed to create an opportunity for me.

I simply could not face up to the painful anxiety. I fixed the problem in the grip of OCD but I feel a looming anxiety still hanging over my head.

I am having anxiety about the future. I am worried about my financial situation in the upcoming weeks. I have a psychiatrist appointment with a new doctor which is driving me nuts. I feel bad that I was forced to put all my medication into uncontaminated paper cups instead of leaving them in their original contaminated bottles. I feel I have missed an opportunity to grow. "Where do I go from here?" "Where do I grow from here?" I need to let go of all this shit and simply be at peace. I need to be peace. If I am anxious I am then being anxiety. I do not want this to be my reality. I need to be the conqueror of my demons. I need to be my own hero.

3-9-10

My problems are serious but trivial compared to the era last year when I was seriously suicidal. However, despite that, my pain in the 'present moment' is all I can feel now in the 'present moment' no matter how trivial the pain is. Last night I went out with my sister. Before going out I had a premonition that it might not be the best idea, but I chose to go out anyway. We went to a crowded club and I a suffered a major panic attack. It was obvious that I was having a horrible experience. I sat in the corner of the club for most of the night until my sister and I decided to go home early. The whole experience left me feeling so depressed. I kept asking myself why? Why did I go out? I should have stayed in. I went home later that night but the anxiety and regret remained. I was finally able to fall asleep for a few hours, but at 4:00 A.M. I woke up in a panic. How awful. I tossed and turned for hours until I had to say "screw it" and got the hell out of bed. The only activity I could think of was to exercise and I did. It felt good to get the body moving and the blood flowing. I hopped in the shower and began my day early. I left my apartment at approximately 7:00 A.M. The significance of these events is that, positively speaking, I turned a gut wrenching situation into a bright new morning. I am figuring out ways to turn shit into gold. Also, I had not seen sunlight in days!

What really irked me the wrong way at the club last night was that I had placed my jacket on a couch in the corner of the club which felt safe, but this couch was located right near the D.J. booth. What occurred next was horrifying. A woman climbed onto the couch to request a song from the D.J. located above. At first I was simply angry that she had her dirty boots all over the seats my sister and I were sitting on. My sister was dancing at the time. Then I noticed the hell that was being unfolded. The girl had her boots placed right on top of my jacket. AAAHHH! For a person with my type of OCD this is a nightmare. My anxiety was obviously tremendously high. This all occurred after I was already experiencing a panic attack simply from being at the crowded club. I do not know why I write of this other than to expose the symptoms of obsessive-compulsive disorder.

But now I am looking for a new consciousness. A better consciousness. It is time to move on. So I had a horrifying night. My coat is now contaminated, but the positive aspect of this is that I am here alive to write all this down. My hand is moving as I write, which means the signals from my brain to body are intact. This is something to rejoice for. I have more than my pain, my suffering. I have my life, no matter how awful it seems to be at times. It is all my own and I am responsible for it. From suicide to God. I know that God exists because God, the Creator, always gives me the strength to move on. If I could not move on then I would be stuck. Without God I would be in one place for my whole life. Stuck for all my remaining time. But this is not the case. God allows me to move on. Whether or not you believe in God, there is a force behind this all. One which I will never fully understand, but one which I will always be in love with.

I am looking for a new consciousness. Whether or not it includes mental illness and panic attacks or extreme negativity it will be new because I will always know that I have the strength to move on and to grow from my struggles. This alone is a new consciousness. One I did not believe in before, but one I know exists now. I will never quit in seeking this new, vibrant, lovely consciousness. Obstacles will occur but for a reason. To allow me to grow strong. Obstacles are a part of life. For to face obstacles is true living no matter how painful. We all seek peace, but to truly find peace we must accept the chaos and obstacles which are a natural part of life. And to truly live well, we will bravely face these obstacles and survive. This is how we attain peace.

3-9-10

Allow me to explain more clearly what my obsessive-compulsive disorder is. It is true suffering. I force myself to obsessively think about a thought systematically or I force myself to act out an action compulsively. It takes its toll on the mind, soul, and body. I feel that I hold on to this disorder very tightly and that it holds on to me. It feels impossible to let go of. The grip of this disease is so unpredictable and strong. When a negative event occurs or a negative thought occurs which disrupts my comfort zone of OCD the result is extreme panic and anxiety. It is in no way humorous. There is no escape from the anxiety of OCD unless I give into the rituals required of the OCD. I want out of this cycle but it is so hard. I will not quit trying to beat this demon.

My depression is another story. I feel worthlessness and lack of purpose. All I have is my writing but I do not know if it will affect anyone. I want it to. I want everyone going through what I am going through to hold on tight. It is a bumpy ride but we must hold on. There is a reason for this all. God help me! God help us all! I want to achieve this new consciousness but the road blocks are haunting. I need to toughen up.

In a perfect world what would I want? What do I need? I need satisfaction. I need lasting joy. Why can I not have it? Maybe this new consciousness does not include these luxuries. Maybe this new consciousness includes suffering so that I can learn to overcome all the obstacles I am facing. I figured it out! I am always looking for the easy way out but that is not the key. The right road is the hard road. The bumps are there for a reason; for me to jump over them. I must. I must pass through. I'll take the bad. I am tired of being tired. It is time for change. It is always time for change. It is always time for growth.

3-24-10

A new consciousness is what I will attain. I am working so hard to attain this dream of mine. I have been put through the test to an ultimate degree over the past few weeks and I am still standing. There were moments when I really did not think that I was going to make it yet I prevailed. As far as my OCD goes, I have been faced with some of the scariest obstacles possible, but I continue to fight. This is my new battle strategy. Never give up. Never surrender. I am not fooling around anymore. The time has come for me to take my mental illness and run with it. I will not let my mental illness dictate my life; I will dictate my mental illness. I am going through the hardest struggles. Harder than I could ever have imagined but that is the way OCD works. It gets worse and worse until you reach a breaking point. A point of no return. I am determined and furious. There is a good chance that my steam to beat the OCD will wear away but I will get it back because the pain is too intense not to fight in my case. I cannot loose sight of this ever. The pain is so strong even as I write. A weak man would ask, "Why is this happening to me?" But a strong man will ask, "Why am I not defeating this demon?" The stronger the test the harder I will fight.

The most recent test I have been facing has really discouraged me over the last few days. I am not sure how to battle this monster either. There is nothing that I can do to battle it other than to ignore it and sit with the pain. I have to sit with the regret, the frustration, and the suffering. I have to deal with this for the rest of my life no matter what. I am tired of playing the victim role. It is not for me any longer. I used to play the victim and lay in bed day after day hopeless. The sun is shining today. I am making sure of it. I do not care if it is cloudy and raining outside anymore. The sun shall shine around me. I will make sure of this. I am contaminated or so I believe I am; the sun still shines around me. I am stuck in a position of agony and pain; the sun still shines around me. When the day turns to night the illumination of the moon will be my light. No matter where I go from here on in, I will be surrounded by light. Prison is dark and I have been living in it for too long a time. Through the cracks of the prison door I see light. With this light I am prisoner no longer.

I have been blind to see the light for so long now. I have been trapped in my mind for many years. But after years of suffering I am finally ready to make my escape. I will break down the prison walls so that the light will not need to be seen through little cracks any more. There will be no wall at all. Only light. I am ready for this indeed. I am past the point of no return. Fear has been my way of life for too many years now. Power and confidence is finally here to replace that fear. The nightmare has come to a close. If it returns in my dreams again, I will shatter it.

I will suffer again, this I am sure of, but I now understand that I must so that I can grow. Right now as I write these words I still feel a looming sense of doom, but I am prepared for this after all. I have been in training for months now. Training to grab this sickness by the horns and destroy it. The confusing part is that I am not sure whether to always fight the pain or just let it be. Maybe the best way to attack the pain is to simply sit with it and wait for it to dissipate. While doing this I must distract myself with positive thinking. The pain will exist. The pain will always return. It is a matter of how I face the pain which matters.

3-25-10

Another hard day has occurred. Today I started the day out with a good work out followed by a shower. I then went out after getting dressed as usual, but for some strange yet predictable reason I felt that I needed to shower again after I already spent too much time in my first shower. What a drag on my day. I get these urges because of the OCD. My anxiety sky rocketed. I tried my damn hardest to fight; to resist the urge of going back home to shower. I knew in my heart that one shower was enough but my mind kept begging me to go home and shower again. The weather was beautiful but I could not enjoy it because of the anxiety. "Go home. Shower again." This is what the darkness of OCD kept telling me. I tried to tell myself that if I resisted the urge that I would grow to be a better, stronger man. I tried fighting the demon off, but my strength was not enough. I finally gave in. I rushed home, threw off all my clothing, and then hopped back into the shower.

I knew another challenge would come my way. They always do. But why on such a gorgeous day did this agony occur. How annoying. How devastating to my well being. But enough complaining. I can only go forward from here. The OCD won the battle but the war is far from over. The war shall last until my very last breath. This is what mental illness really is. An all out war. I have come to terms with this. This is the reason why I refer to myself as a soul warrior. Any human being going through any hard ship in life is a soul warrior. It does not only have to be mental illness that someone is suffering from. There are plenty of souls fighting their own battles aside from mental illness and they too are soul warriors. Fighting mental illness is just one of the many wars that require a soul warrior to overcome. Mental illness is so excruciatingly hard to defeat, so the soul warrior in us must work extra hard to fight.

So today I lost a hard battle but I am here now ready for the next. I am committed to this war. I am committed to victory. I failed earlier today but I have all intentions of winning from here on. To win however may require loosing at first but then rising above afterwards. Life works in very mysterious ways. I predicted failure yesterday but I knew then what the most important aspect of failure is; how one reacts to it. What can one learn from falling down? How can one get back up after they hit the ground hard? I will not be discouraged. I am still standing despite my loss earlier today. Whether or not I fail my next test, I know what counts the most is how I react to the outcome. I must stand tall as a soul warrior.

3-26-10

Where do I grow from here? I still find myself terrified by the future. I cannot fully comprehend that the now is all that exists. The concept of the future is the perfect outlet leading too worry. All my worry exists while thinking of upcoming events and moments in the future. The future frightens me. So much can go wrong. What can I do to fully understand that the future is just an imaginary dream or in my case a nightmare. My past is a concept full of regret; my future worry. Why does it have to be so hard for me to stay centered in the now? Why is it so hard for me to stay centered in the present moment? Literally speaking, I live in the present moment always. The essence of me exists in the present moment only, but my mind tries to waver into the future and imagines all that can go wrong in it.

If I am able to comprehend this idea now in the present moment than I need to put into practice all I have just written down. The reason it is so hard to live in the present moment is because of a detachment from our souls. The soul is constantly striving to be located right in the middle of the now. The soul is what yearns for the present moment and the present moment only. When I am busy obsessing and agonizing about the past and future my soul does not want anything to do with this worry. It is as if I am unintentionally stretching out my soul in ways it does not want to be stretched. My soul wants peace. I believe my mind does as well, but I have a disorder where my mind is constantly focused and obsessed with what is not the present moment. I will not find any peace in focusing only on the future and I will not find peace obsessing about the past. I will find peace in the present. This does not mean I cannot peacefully dream about the future and enjoy reminiscing about the past. It means that I cannot get stuck in the future or the past. When you are stuck somewhere which does not even exist then pain arises.

3-29-10

Today is a rainy Monday afternoon in Brookline. My Obsessive-compulsive disorder is stable at the moment but I am prepared for it to get worse. In regards to my OCD, anything that touches the ground is automatically contaminated. Earlier today, I carelessly dropped my umbrella right onto the ground. But I noticed something new. The anxiety only remained for a few seconds. Instead of freaking out about the obsessive-compulsive mishap, I tried to stay calm. I picked up the umbrella, got a few napkins, and simply wiped the visible dirt off. I felt satisfied after that action.

I have been working hard to limit my anxiety after an event takes place which negatively affects my OCD. To be on top of sky rocketing anxiety is extremely complicated. Your wits go numb because of the anxiety and pain. You forget all that you have already learned about how to combat the disorder. All you have are two options in the present moment; to die or to live. To die would be to throw out the umbrella because it is contaminated. To live would be to keep the contaminated umbrella. This reminds me of a humorous story which occurred only a week ago. It happened to be a rainy day, like today. I had to urinate badly and could not go all the way to my apartment to handle my business. I decided that the best place to go would be one of the local coffee shops nearby. I rushed into the restroom but had forgotten to remove my backpack before entering. My umbrella was placed in a small side compartment on my bag. I began my business and then all hell broke loose. Clank! I heard the sound of misery and looked down. My umbrella had fallen right out of my backpack onto the bathroom floor right by the toilet. I knew there was no hope for the poor umbrella. I looked at it sitting there on top of some discarded toilet paper and then looked away. The umbrella was not mine any longer. It was unusable. I then left the bathroom angry but calm, went to the local drug store and bought a new umbrella. To be honest, this unfortunate story is quite humorous. I am now able to find some humor even in the worst case scenerios.

The lesson of the story is not clear cut because I did leave the umbrella on the bathroom floor. There was no way I would dare touch the umbrella after it fell on top of pure contamination. However, in this case I believe most people would be rather disgusted with the unfortunate fall of the umbrella. The only good that came out of this nasty event is that I did remain calm and can now see some humor in the situation because the situation is literally one of my worst OCD nightmares. When a worst case scenario plays out sometimes the best thing to do is to chuckle. But again, I would like to remind the reader that OCD is no laughing matter.

3-29-10

It seems to me that there is a whole lot of irony in this universe of ours. A lot of bad events take place but for what reason? Many negative events feel like coincidences which makes me so angry. But what if these negative occurrences are placed in front of us not by coincidence but by fate. A fate alive and real there to play out a very important function; to test us. These obstacles which seem so annoying and unreasonable just may be there to better ourselves. To make ourselves that much stronger and tougher. What if every OCD mishap is meant to be? These mishaps are a part of our fate put there by God. This is the best outlook one suffering from obsessive-compulsive disorder can achieve. I plan on keeping this positive outlook to combat my OCD and to live with peace of mind.

3-30-10

I love to begin some writing sessions with a question. Today I will ask an important one which I have asked before. Where do I grow from here? I had a tough night sleeping. I went to bed at around midnight, tossed and turned for hours, and then saw that the time was 5:00 A.M. Instead of becoming furious at my lack of rest, I instead thought more positively about the problem. Another early morning adventure I thought. Why not? I don't need a full night of sleep. At least my body got to lie down for a good, long five hours. So where do I grow from here?

I decided to meet up with a wonderful, dear friend of mine who I cherish. He was on his way to class so at around 8:00 A.M. we met at a coffee shop. This friend of mine happens to be going through some very complicated issues. Getting into a good school and appeasing his family are examples. These are serious concerns on his plate. Another huge worry he has is that he is gay in a world which is not accepting of this lifestyle. I love this friend who really is more mature than any man I know. I would die for him. However, he has been depressed because to be 'out' in this world creates a dilemma. Many gay men his age are not yet ready to admit their sexual orientation. Because of this he is having a hard time finding a boyfriend. I try to be as supportive as possible but even I know that when you are looking for love and cannot find it life can seem quite dreary. If I could, I would set him up with a man worthy of my friend, but finding one is complicated.

The main problem is that he blames his trouble finding a significant other on himself which is extremely unhealthy. He is one of the most handsome guys I know. His artistic talent is out of this world. He has so many gifts that he can share with the world, but first he is looking for a significant other to share himself with. As his best friend, I support him one-hundred percent and want so badly for him to find a worthy lover. This young man who is my dearest friend deserves it more than anyone in the world. His potential is endless.

As I gain control over my own issues, I am starting to open up and realize other people's issues and problems. This is good because it puts me in a position where I can offer myself to help others and to share my essence with a person in need. I feel I have a lot to offer another human being in regards to personal problems. The great thing is that as I fight and beat my mental afflictions, I am opening myself up more and more to help others. This is the most fulfilling action and service a human can provide for another human.

Life can be beautiful if you allow yourself to see it this way. It all depends on how you look at your struggles. Do not always rely on life to go as planned to determine the quality of your current situation. The tougher the better. The tougher your situation is the more room for growth there is and this answers my original question: Where do I grow from here? I grow from the toughest situations and end up in the best situations. I grow to become a better man. The man I was born to become all along. From hell we rise to Heaven. This is possible!

3-30-10

Positive thinking is a philosophy that has been practiced from the beginning of man's intellect I am sure, but for many individuals in today's world to stay positive is extremely hard and complicated. Life is not simple for anyone whether you want to believe it or not. Even the most privileged individuals have to deal with the concept of mortality. This concept can be very disturbing. Staying positive or thinking positively in my opinion is a skill that must be practiced and achieved. I believe the hardest part about achieving this desirable skill is that we all must fall. It is our nature as human beings to fall. This is what God has intended for us. If we did not fall no lessons would be learned and no growth would be made by anyone. But falling obviously hurts so to get back up immediately and simply shake it off is not always realistic. It is a challenge. A challenge most of us face daily. I face falling hourly or even by the minute usually. The key is to take the time to assess the situation. Think about your options after you have fallen. Think about what you truly desire after the fall. Do you want to move closer to death or closer to life. To remain on the ground is to move closer to death. To get back up, which is certainly the harder of the two, is the action of moving closer to life. The skill of rising after the fall is the skill of positive thinking which is also positive action. It is easier said than done but the only way to test this theory is to practice it once on the ground.

3-30-10

Retraining my brain is the biggest yet most important challenge I will ever have to face but it can be done. It is not easy. As a matter of fact it is the hardest challenge of my life. I have been suffering from obsessive-compulsive disorder and depression for so many years now. I wonder what it will take to undue all of this negativity. Will I have to work on retraining my brain for the same amount of years that I have been a victim to mental illness? This scares me obviously. There are a lot of years to be made up for. I am hoping that with faith in God I can undue the damage in a shorter amount of time than it took to become so sick. In other words, I hope that if I fight hard enough against the darkness that I will undue the damage quicker than it took for the damage to become so severe. This is what I pray for and I will not quit. Even if I have to fight for as long as I have suffered I will still stay in the fight, in the war, determined to excel and to win. *It is not about curing my mental illness. It is about beating my mental illness.*

4-2-10

The day started off great. The weather perfect. However, what goes up must come down. When I feel good I usually predict that soon enough the joy will dissipate. I am quite used to this after so many years of being sick. After enjoying the warm weather for a few hours and going to therapy, I sat down at a Mexican restaurant for lunch. After this the day went sour. I have a strong phobia of trash and dumpsters. On my way home after lunch I saw that the maintenance man in my building was elbow deep in the dumpster located in the back of the building's garage. I was going home to get my new laptop and feared that on the way out of my building I would come into contact with the maintenance man. I was right. When I was out the door of my building we crossed paths. He did not touch me but he came close enough to me where I felt that because he had been contaminated I was now contaminated. When we crossed paths I was carrying my laptop. My anxiety went up because I felt as though my new laptop was now contaminated. AAAHHH!

But the sun is still shining and as I write I cannot let this event of contamination get the best of me. There is a better way out of this mind trap. I need to understand that just because I crossed paths with the maintenance man, this does not automatically mean that my laptop and my body are contaminated. I need to wake up and stop this nonsense thinking. My laptop is fine. It is not contaminated. Better yet, so what if it is contaminated. This would be better for my OCD. To beat OCD you must attack it. If I fear being contaminated then I should allow myself to be contaminated and deal with it. I cannot surrender to a mental disease. I must win. Defeat the enemy. My mental affliction is the enemy. It must be destroyed. This is the positive way of thinking. The only way to be a soul warrior is to deal with the pain and accept it. Live with it. A soul warrior must remain calm and collected. A soul warrior must remain positive. A soul warrior never surrenders to the pain that the mind creates.

OCD affects the mind and the soul but I feel its home is in the mind. I can look at this war as mind vs. soul; however that is not the only way to fight. Even though the mind falls victim to the OCD it can still be used as a weapon. My soul gives me strength to fight and so can the mind. It is as if my mind is divided and I need to put my faith in the sane portion. As long as I allow my soul to remain strong I can use my mind as a tactical weapon in this war. After all, it takes both the mind and soul to remain positive. To remain positive is to win this war.

4-2-10

Life starts from here. Every second is a new moment. Every moment a new second. I have wasted many years suffering but now I have decided to change it all around. Yes there is plenty of pain in my past which lurks behind me, but I am learning to manage it. The past hurts, but it is over once and for all. Life begins from here.

Tomorrow frightens me. I do not know how it will come and what it will hand me, but again, worrying about the future is counterproductive. Time is like a ghost here to scare us all. If time were no issue could you imagine the peace? Finally, I am able to stay and hover in the now!

4-2-10

It is time to man up. No more feeling sorry for myself. I must accept that life is a lonesome journey. I often find myself wondering the streets all by myself even though I know so many people. I choose this path I guess. I feel lonely, but that is life. When we die we die alone. Get used to the loneliness. This is the best way to live. No more being dependent on others for my enjoyment of life. I have always been so reliant on the approval of others, but no more. I will ride this journey alone and love it. To embrace loneliness is the hardest part of life but it is a must to being spiritually successful.

I find myself terrified by rejection but why? I am dependent on the judgment and approval of others. This cannot last if I want to live a fulfilling life. Other humans will not dictate the quality of my life any longer. This is true strength. To live alone, proudly and without shame. Shame is poison. Poison for the mind, soul, and spirit. The combination of mind, soul, and spirit is consciousness. I will strengthen my mind, soul, and spirit right now so that I will have a better, stronger consciousness. This is the beautiful life. It can be mine. It can be yours. This is the miracle of life. The miracle is that we can shape our own lives. I was at a point exactly one year ago where I was sure I had nothing left. I contemplated taking it all away, but now I am a new man. I rebuilt my mind to where it is now in the present moment. I rebuilt my soul to where it is now in the present moment. I rebuilt my spirit to where it is now in the present moment. I rebuilt my life to where it is now in the present moment. Existence is a blessing not a curse. We will all die. This is why it is so beautiful to live well in the present moment.

4-5-10

I am not quite sure where to go from here. I am in a better place than where I was one year ago but I still feel unfulfilled. I want more to write. I want more to express. I want to share with the world who I am and all the possibilities that approach me. I can do more with my life. I know it. Am I not trying hard enough? What more can I do to live a good life. To live with God. I want to live with God. This is where I belong. This is what I long for. But there are just so many obstacles and distractions in the way. I am going to assume that everything happens for a reason and that these distractions are put in front of us so that we can conquer them and rise above where we were before, thus bringing us closer to the creator of all. This must be the truth. Truth is what I am seeking. Truth only. I am getting to old to live in a lie. An illusion. My illusion is my ego and this is what I must destroy.

The truth is that I am so depressed. I am trying to remain positive through this down fall but it remains to be very hard. To stay positive while you feel like shit is like a chore. Imagine feeling worthless and without prospect. This is my current reality. I know that I have made some breakthrough progress in the past few weeks but I am feeling low again. I guess that this is the test I have been predicting to happen. When positive, I am aware that I will fall again and that it is crucial for me to get back up. Well right now I am in the funk so it is so important that I get through this hell and do what I must to remain positive enough. I certainly am trying but every face I see on the street makes me sadder. I want to enjoy this life given to me but there is too much pain involved. Again, my obsession with the future still haunts me. This I must get over but I am so preoccupied with feelings of fear and doubt about how I will survive in the future. How bad will my OCD be? Will I be able to get out of bed? Will I still remain haunted? These questions linger and destroy my present moment. My now. I have been through this time and time again. What do I need to do to become strong enough not to worry? Do I need to pray harder? Do I need to do more for others? My actions now dictate this concept of my future so what should I be doing different? A lot still needs to change and only I can make the difference. The difference must take place in the present moment. My life depends on this!

I don't know what else to write. I am unhappy yet would like to be happy. This describes so many people suffering in this world obviously. I am just one of the millions. But I want to figure out a way to defeat the disease of unhappiness. Lack of satisfaction does not have to be real. I can taste this. I am not going to quit now. I am only having a bad day. Tomorrow will come and save my life. Now I am using this concept of the future for my own advantage. I can live with pain which leads to being stuck or I can live without pain which leads to being free. This is my choice. This choice is also yours. I dream of living happy, joyfully, peacefully, and without regret. I sometimes feel that this is impossible, but why? Too many bad memories I guess…Well it is time to create new memories. It is time to create new life.

4-6-10

Why does everything have to be a chore? With obsessive-compulsive disorder, all the actions that I must perform on a day to day basis are all chores. Chores which must be completed perfectly. The pain of compulsively washing ones own self is excruciating if you are doing so in an obsessive manner. What can be even worse is the pain associated with dissecting a thought or having to repeat mental thoughts obsessively and compulsively in your head. Recently I have been going through some rather sad obsessions and compulsions. What this entails is that I have a negative thought, for example something horrible happening to someone I know, and then to undue the imagery and prevent the occurrence from actually happening I must obsessively and compulsively repeat prayers in my head. This symptom of OCD is far different than my contamination fears. Or is it? In a manner of thinking, whenever I have these morbid, scary thoughts, I feel as if my whole life and psyche are contaminated. I must say the prayers either out loud or in my head. I could not imagine not doing these prayers repetitively. I feel that they will undue the imagined bad occurrences from happening. Sure these prayers come in the form of mental tasks, but they give me comfort after they are completed. The downside is that once they are completed, shortly down the road another bad thought will appear and I will have to go through the prayers all over again. It is a very repetitive cycle which I am having a hard time breaking.

What is OCD? It is a defense mechanism to avoid bad things from happening. It takes the form of a disorder because it becomes more important than all other aspects in one's life.

It holds on to you so tightly and will try never to let go. The more one gives in, the stronger the hold is. The hold is strong enough where one's day to day functioning is greatly hindered. There is a difference between obsessive-compulsive tendencies and obsessive-compulsive disorder. Obsessive-compulsive tendencies do not necessarily get in the way of one's functioning. Some manage to get through their life successfully with these obsessive-compulsive tendencies. They may be important to complete but unless these actions or thoughts get in the way of your life to the point where you cannot function properly anymore, they are only obsessive-compulsive tendencies. Once the actions or thoughts hinder your ability to function properly in life then the obsessive-compulsive tendencies become a disorder. There is a difference.

I have a full blown disorder. My day to day functioning is hindered to the point of excruciating pain. The anxiety I suffer on a day to day basis is unreasonable. I am unable to keep a job or complete school, not because of a lack of motivation or desire, but because I have severe obsessive-compulsive disorder. Plain and simple. I wish my life could be different and so I am trying my hardest to fight the OCD and change my life for the better. I have a good idea of how to break down my OCD. OCD may be a condition I am going to battle until the day I die, so what I can aim to do is turn the obsessive-compulsive disorder into obsessive-compulsive tendencies. I would settle for this. It would be far better than the situation I am in now. I must never loose sight of the fact that I am seeking a new consciousness. This is an appropriate step in achieving this goal.

4-8-10

My obsessive-compulsive disorder reached a bad point yesterday. It was so bad that I could not bear to write of it then. I avoid shaving for one specific reason. When I shave my face I become very obsessive, compulsive, and precise. But yesterday while shaving, I could not stop with the grooming until it felt exactly right. To simplify the matter, I took the situation to such a drastic point where I began to literally bleed from scraping the shaving blade against my skin too many times. This happens quite often. When I start something, anything, my OCD takes control and I then loose control. It is a darn shame what happened yesterday and it ruined my mood thereafter. My face has healed, but my psyche still hurts.

This is very common with OCD. I tend to overdue actions to the point of pain. To the point of blood. While washing my hands, I have cut my fingers with my fingernails and my hands often bleed because I wash them so often. This is a part of the life. I hate it and yet I still accept it as a reality. Well its permanence must end right now. I must not make this mistake again. Please God, do not allow me to make this type of mistake again. Simple tasks that a normal person can do so easily create such a heavy burden on my life, psyche, and soul. What the hell! I won't accept this any longer.

How many times am I going to write and complain about the same repetitive nonsense? How many times am I going to fall victim to this lifestyle of obsessive-compulsive disorder. To the reader this all may seem boring by now. To me it is repetitive as well. So why do I continue to write. Well because I know that someone out there relates to this repetitive nonsense. This hell exists for someone else. I know this for sure, and I am trying to reach out to this soul. I want to say to this brother or sister that you are not alone. That there is someone out there today, right now, this second, suffering the same disorder. I am suffering the same disease and it is horrifying. Please God help us because it is so hard to help ourselves. I will continue to try and fight however.

How many more steps can I take? I am working hard but clearly not hard enough because I still fall prey to the OCD. When will it end I ask? When will it end? Maybe never. But why does this disorder not dissipate? I have figured out so much about it all. I have done the research. I have learned the tricks, yet it still haunts me this very moment. I crave a difference right now. Is it in my power or not? That is the question.

I am tired of writing in such a negative manner. It is time to switch gears. It is time to do better. If you suffer from OCD or depression and want to beat it then you probably understand how circular the system is. Warrior one day and victim the other.

4-9-10

I woke today feeling miserable. What a surprise.... But despite this fact I made an effort to remove the feelings of pain. I hopped out of bed and immediately began to do my routine workout which is actually beginning to become very compulsive. But this helped me feel more empowered. It gave me a sense that I am in control of my situation. Working out the body is a good way of ignoring the mind. A mind which aches and nags at any opportunity. After the workout I jumped into the shower, which to be honest was quite unpleasant. My OCD in the shower was worse than usual. My showers are never pleasant, but I took this shower to a whole new level of systematic pain. After I wash each body part in the shower I force myself to wash my hands so that they are clean to wash the next body part. It takes a fair amount of time and this is why I call my showers systematic. Eventually the shower ended. I then dried off and got dressed which was not too unpleasant. Before taking my medication I obviously washed my hands and then it was time to begin the rest of my day.

It is a rainy Friday afternoon in Brookline. I am sitting in my favorite coffee shop where I do most of my writing. I feel slightly depressed but overall I am somewhat content. I have some important errands to run at 6:00 P.M. which are frightening me to a degree, but I plan on facing them with my head up high. Usually any errand I plan on accomplishing that must take place in the future frightens me. When you have an anxiety disorder as extreme as mine, usually anything that is not happening in the present moment, but instead is planned to take place in the future, is extremely pain provoking and fear-provoking. As a man I am embarrassed to write of all my pain and to write so openly about all that frightens me, but this book is my dream and I am willing to put myself on the line for it. Not only for myself but more importantly for the reader.

As you already know I am a very self conscious human being. I recently was rejected by a girl who I had developed strong feelings for just by staring at her when ever I had the chance to. I hope that this does not make me sound like a sociopath, but this is how a crush is developed. I asked this girl out and she responded by telling me that she was busy. When I heard her excuse to blow me off it was as if a bolder had been chucked right into my stomach. I will never forget how horrible this feeling was. I really thought that I had a chance with this girl. That is why it hurt so much. The pain of rejection is immense. My God, I felt worthless because I now knew I was worth nothing to this girl. My world had been crushed. I was full of self hatred for introducing myself to this girl in the first place. I am so sensitive to the opinion of others that I let this girl who I did not even know destroy my world. I began obsessing about the scenario of the rejection again and again, obsessively and compulsively. I played it all out over and over again in my head like a scene from a movie that kept replaying the same tragic situation. I felt sick with anxiety and shame. My depression was so severe that I was paralyzed internally. OCD does not only affect me in regards to contamination and fears of horrible things happening. OCD also forces me to obsess about certain life situations that have occurred in the 'past' to an extremely compulsive degree. OCD also forces me to obsess about upcoming 'future' life events to an extremely compulsive degree. To simplify this, OCD lives in my past and future and kills my 'present moment.'

4-12-10

Ok. I have taken up too much time complaining about how tough my life is and how negatively the OCD is affecting me. Well, I would like to take this opportunity to change the focus around into something better. I have been speaking of this new, better consciousness for some time now. It is now time to put this new philosophy on life into order. When it is too cold outside I will not take for granted that it could be colder. When it is too hot outside I will not take for granted that it could be hotter. When I feel pain I know that the pain could be greater. I must accept the now for what it is without complaint. I am trying to beat a psychological disorder and I need stronger tactics to do so.

My writing will never do to justice the torment of a psychological disorder, but bear with me, I am trying to deal with and fight the torment. Up until now however I have been very negative with bits and pieces of optimism. Well now I shall up my optimism, which is courageous. The torment is a test. A blessing in disguise. The torment will lead me to something better. I am ready to change my attitude. Welcome to the new me.

4-12-10

God is great. God has given me life. I am here now today. I am here now in the present moment which is forever. I am alive forever. As long as I am breathing, I am then alive forever. What a blessing I have. We are all blessed with this journey. The journey is hard but it is none the less a blessing. A gift. Take it. By participating in your own life you are winning your own life. These are the rules of the game. If you choose to loose, you loose, but the loss is a blessing. If you choose to win then you win, and the victory is a blessing. We are all blessed with chance. We are all blessed with life.

4-12-10

So my life is now changed. It is in my own power to do this. To switch the gears of my life. The life I have been living has been too hard. Let me explain to you some more symptoms of my OCD. Recently I have been getting over a huge fear of mine. *'The fear of getting others sick.'* I had been struggling with this issue for a long time. I had been constantly worried that I unintentionally was going to get a loved one tragically ill. Some how.... I was worried that I would pick up super-bacteria on my hands and spread it to my family and cause the worst case scenario possible. And it would be my entire fault. The guilt would obviously be immense. I thought I was going to really harm a loved one through contamination. This fear really ran my life for a while. To prevent getting loved ones sick I would go through extra measures to make sure my hands were always clean. Obviously I would obsessively and compulsively wash them more than necessary. I come from a large family with many young children, more susceptible to illness than adults. I was consumed with a fear that I would cause one of my little nieces or nephews to become sick with a life-threatening illness. This type of a worry is more crucial than the whole universe to me, so one can imagine the devastating effect it had on my psyche.

Another fear I had to beat was *'the fear of starting a fire.'* This particular fear caused me to worry that I would accidentally cause a fire, killing innocent people, especially my loved ones. I believed that the cause of the fire would be from leaving on an electrical appliance or light which would malfunction thus, creating a fire. I still have issues with this to this day. It is not as bad as it used to be however. I remember being in my family's home not sure whether or not I had turned off a light. Clearly the light would be shut off, but the OCD caused me to question this to such a ridiculous and painful point. I would stand there paralyzed constantly checking if the light was really off. I would tell myself that maybe it was still on and that my mind was tricking me into believing that the light was off. My mind was definitely playing tricks on me; that's for sure. I would just stand there, obsessively and compulsively staring at the turned off light. Even today after turning off a light I still stare so intensely at the bulb to make sure it is off, even though the strong side off me is already sure it is. However the weak side of me cannot stop checking.

I do these actions of checking with all sorts of electrical objects including space heaters, fans, televisions, computers, and everything else that can potentially start a fire. I try to avoid cooking because I am so scared that I will some how leave the stove on and end up being responsible for innocent lives lost in flames. I am not so worried about my own death, but I am deeply concerned for the welfare of others.

I obviously have a serious 'checking disorder.' Another checking problem I have is with locks. I always compulsively check to make sure that I have correctly locked any door I am shutting which needs to be locked. This compulsion is especially strong when I am leaving my family's home. When I leave my family's home I get consumed with worry that somehow I will not correctly lock the door. I then imagine a lunatic walking in to the house, God forbid. I will stand there like a maniac just checking to make sure the door is locked. I need to be sure of it. I cannot leave without completing the obsessive-compulsive action. I have to do this until it feels right. Until the obsessive-compulsive voice in my head is satisfied. These are the worries OCD causes. It is no laughing matter. It is however mental and spiritual torture.

4-12-10

My OCD is so strong that it is beginning to affect even my writing. After every section I write, I obsessively and compulsively force my self to check each sentence to make sure all is well. This is a very light symptom of the OCD. It gets so much worse than that so I should not complain. I simply find it annoying. That's all. I need to make sure that this symptom does not grow because writing is a very important passion for me. I want the OCD to let go. I want to let go of the OCD. I am learning. Slowly, but surely, I am learning.

I have had this disorder since I was so young. I barely remember life without it. I was about twelve or maybe eleven when I first started developing the symptoms. I still remember my first obsessive-compulsive symptom. I would have to knock on wood in patterns of four to prevent bad events from occurring. I shared a room with my brother then. The knocking would go on and on through out the night. It would keep my brother awake. He would become very annoyed by it but I just could not stop. I would have to keep knocking in sets of four. Writing about it makes me feel a bit sick.

4-13-10

It is time to stop beating around the bush. Some serious pain has been thrown my way because of the OCD. When I was a teen, I was involuntarily hospitalized many times. My symptoms were misunderstood as psychotic and not obsessive-compulsive. What I saw in the psych wards was very disturbing. I spent time in children's psych wards which in its self is disturbing, and I spent time in adult psych wards which would blow your mind away. Some of the characters I saw in those wards were extremely psychotic. It was disturbing to be locked up in there and it still bothers me to this day. It was a very sad scene. I still remember when I was seventeen, being involuntarily locked up and being extremely disturbed by the lack of freedom. I became agitated and began asking the head nurse of the hospital unit why I was there and I was telling her that I did not belong there. After questioning the situation for some time the nurse then became annoyed and angry and ordered me into a room. After a few minutes of sitting in the room the nurse reentered with too very large gentleman in black suits. The nurse then told me that I had to take a pill. I refused. She then told me that if I did not take the pill orally then it would be administered into my body by force against my will. I became scared, being so young, and agreed to take the pill. I was knocked out almost instantaneously. I did not wake up until the following morning. At least the nurse did not have me around agitating her any longer.

4-15-10

I have had it up to here. Today was an unfortunate one so far. My hands became contaminated early in the day which spoiled my mood. I had therapy which was dreadful because for the whole session all I could think about was taking another shower in an attempt to restart the day. A new beginning. The shower would serve as a cleansing process. I asked my therapist to let me go early so that I could rush home and shower. The reason that I was so intent on re-showering was because my day started off tarnished. Damaged. Early on I contaminated my hands and because I had to perform a washing ritual to fix the problem, I felt like a weak, little man. I wanted a new beginning. So I finally reached home and showered. I felt a bit better. OCD is like a drug. Your mind tricks you into feeling like you need to perform an obsessive compulsive action. You want to do it so badly; like getting high. And then you take the hit of the drug which is performing the OCD ritual. After you successfully complete a ritual you do get a relieving high but then, like a drug, you crash because lurking around the corner is another horrible ritual waiting to be completed.

So I have related being addicted to drugs with obsessive-compulsive disorder. I have done all sorts of drugs so I know that there are similarities. Living with OCD is as unhealthy to the psyche, soul, and spirit as drugs are to the body. They both run and ruin your life and the better side of you wishes to live without the affliction. This is just an observation.

It is about time I stop concentrating on the OCD and move on to a brighter side of life. I will always be searching for that new consciousness. I will never give that up.

4-16-10

I feel that I am most susceptible to OCD in the morning time while getting ready for the day. Today after showering I began washing my hands again. I noticed that I had washed my hands to a point where a small, visible cut had developed underneath my right index finger's nail. It was bleeding slightly so I began to panic. I do not like having cuts on my hand where blood can easily get onto my clothing or anything else for that matter. For example my new laptop; I would not like blood to spread onto my laptop because then I would have to obsessively-compulsively clean it off with disinfecting wipes or maybe wet paper towel. Can you believe it?! My OCD has me frightened of my own blood. Ridiculous I know...Anyway. I digress. Back to the cut underneath my right index finger's nail. I waited for it to stop bleeding. After the bleeding had stopped I began to wash my hands again very neurotically. I washed the minor cut's blood away and then felt better but the process was not quite over.

After washing my hands I had to wait for them to dry. Then came the lotioning process. Because I wash my hands so much, I make sure to apply moisturizing lotion onto my hands after most washes. If I did not do this my hands would become extremely dry from over soaping and over washing. I do this very systematically. Palm, fist, fingers, nails....It must go perfectly. After the lotioning was done I then felt ready to go on with my day which has led me here. Writing about today's annoying events.

I understand that if you do not suffer from OCD or some sort of psychological disorder, what I am writing about may not seem like a big deal. But allow me to explain the distress little bits of OCD causes; even insignificant occurrences like a small, superficial cut. I believe a severe panic is created and that it affects the central nervous system. Your body physically changes from relaxed to stressed. Your muscles tighten. Your breathing becomes shortened and less deep, creating a suffocation feeling. The most noticeable physical change however is the change in heart beat. My heart begins to race harder and faster as each second passes. The anxiety creates this fast, pounding heart beat. Both psychologically and physically, OCD has me beat. It really does affect the mind, soul, spirit, and body in a very extreme and negative way.

4-21-10

It is absolutely amazing how strong the pull of OCD is. I actually had a great day but it was stolen by this monster. I spent the morning playing basketball alone which was so relaxing. I then had some nice conversation with my mother and brother at the local coffee shop. All was well or so it seemed. The pull of OCD took me down in the early evening following the pleasant day. The way the sickness grabbed hold of me was very dramatic and sickening. At least I got through most of the day successfully however. I only have one option and that is to look at the situation positively. I was torn to pieces this early evening, but now at this night I am able to write about the ordeal as a situation gone and lost in the past. Life keeps moving so I must remember to keep moving with it. Even if I become derailed I need to always get back on track. I will make it somehow. I must.

4-22-10

Today was a good day. I practiced some exposure therapy. I have an issue with purchasing sanitary items; for example soap, paper towel, toilet paper, shampoo…basically anything I need to stay uncontaminated. Before purchasing any of these products I perform a hand washing ritual. However today I bit the bullet. I felt motivated. I thought to myself, the hell with this OCD. With unwashed hands I did what I had to do to fight my obsessive-compulsive disorder. I bought sanitary products with my dirty hands and plan on using the items without throwing them away, which I have done many a time in the past. It feels good. For a normal person this is no accomplishment, but for me it is indeed. I feel that I am beginning to attack the OCD more and more. Stronger and harder. I plan on winning more battles so that this war will be in my favor. If I fall I will attack harder and allow the pain of the fall to strengthen me. I have what it takes. OCD has run my life for too long now and I am ready to let it go forever. This will be the hardest goal I will ever have to complete but I feel that I was born to do it. I was born to succeed.

4-23-10

It is an early hour of April 23, 2010. Just after 4:00 A.M. and I am still awake. I actually do not see myself sleeping for some time. I do not really care. So I'll wake up late. I am a night owl. I do love the day though; especially the glory of the sun. My OCD is under control right now along with my depression. I could write down some negative information of the night's events which bothered me but that would only bore you. I had a couple of contamination episodes but managed to get through them. I am only going to write about the positive side of life.

I have a lot to look forward to. I have been so distracted by my mental issues to a point where I forget the meaning of optimism. I am turning twenty-seven soon which is fairly young. I have life left and I plan to enjoy it. I feel more inspired to live well these days. My writing has been serving me so productively in a very therapeutic way. I find it helpful to write down my life situation so that I can look at it objectively. When I do this I know that I can survive. Writing allows me the ability to be able to look at the big picture and understand that there is hope.

I am content to be providing myself the freedom to enjoy life. My mental illness has stripped me of my freedom so to feel free again is so beautiful and enjoyable. I have come to terms with being sick but I have not come to terms with a lack of freedom. That I will not tolerate.

4-25-10

It is amazing how much stress little chores cause me. Just simple day to day functioning creates pain for me. If I have to clean my apartment or pick something up from the store, I will drive myself crazy thinking about it. I am becoming more positive and I am living more free, but I cannot lie and pretend that my OCD and depression are gone. I feel overwhelmed by life. What still bothers me the most are the days to come. These days are where the little chores and routine functioning lie which still frighten me. I need to grab hold of myself and stop becoming overwhelmed by life. Right now my kitchen is a mess and I know that I must clean it, but instead of cleaning it right away I am only obsessing about it and overwhelming myself. I need to understand that there is a better way to live. Either I can clean it now or I can forget about it and do it later. Obsessively worrying about the upcoming event will do no good but only create chaos and harm. I will only become overwhelmed and this is not the way to live.

4-28-10

Depression is crippling. It is extremely hard to fight. Even if you are around many people, you still feel all alone. When you are stuck on the ground it is a complicated process to get back up. Millions suffer from depression. All suffer in varying degrees. I suffer from major depression and it comes at me hard and strong. One day can be seemingly pleasant but then by night I am stuck in a dark hole. What can one do to combat depression? Depression is a demon in full form.

When I am depressed I try my hardest to see the brighter side of life. It is April and beautiful flowers are beginning to bloom. It is drizzling outside which can be seen as annoying but today the beauty of these new flowers are blinding me from the slight aggravation of the rain. On a street by the corner where my apartment is located the whole sidewalk was covered by beautiful, pink flower petals that had fallen from their blooming mother tree. When I quietly walked over the petals I felt as if I was in heaven. It was only for a split second, but I am so grateful for that beautiful moment. Moments like these help combat depression.

Another sign of my severe depression is my recreational drug usage. I guess the reason I do drugs, like drinking and smoking pot, is to escape the pain of life. However, often these drugs increase the pain and depression. Drugs give me a short period of satisfaction but they always leave me feeling empty. If I were not depressed would I use drugs? Am I depressed because I use drugs? I believe it is a little bit of both, however drugs aside, I believe my depression has biological roots and would exist either way. Sometimes the drugs do give me short occurrences of euphoria which I love, but it is such a nasty habit to always be around them and to be dependent upon them.

I have had a problem with addiction for many years now. I believe the reason for this is because when you are on drugs it feels as if life is being lived for you. The drugs are leading you on a journey and you need not put in any effort. It sounds fun, but eventually the ride comes to an end. This is why the answer is not to be reliant on drugs. I must figure out a way to enjoy life passionately without substance abuse in the picture. This is challenging for a man prone to addiction. I must admit that reality frightens me.

From now on I need to begin chasing those split second occurrences with nature's beauty like with the flower petals. This is how I will combat depression. I will enjoy little, split second pieces of heaven that are in everyone's ability to find if you only search. I am going to combat my depression by appreciating. The beautiful life can be mine. The beautiful life can be yours. I plan on receiving it from now on. It is a gift but it is also a birthright.

5-1-10

It is the first day of May and it has been more than a year since my psychological breakdown. I made it. I feel great. I am falling in love with life again. I feel the spring air against my skin and smell the spring scent and can finally enjoy it. Thank God for life. There is still negativity in my life but the positive aspects are beginning to outweigh the negative. I will continue on this journey. I will continue to learn. I will continue to survive. This gift of life shall not be taken for granted any longer. I am so grateful.

5-5-10

I am trying so hard to remain positive through these crucial days of my life. They are crucial because they are all I have to hold on to. However, because of my mental illness I am so psychologically fragile. Every chore, errand, or event in my life creates such a burden on my psyche. The future still haunts me. I become so worried about it and have a hard time remaining in the present moment. I am doing well with the past. I am able to overlook it and move on which is a great step to be made. Being disturbed by the past can be very debilitating. I need to grab hold of myself and get over my anxiety of the future. I need to let upcoming events happen gracefully and naturally; not rigidly and forcefully. I need to take better care of myself. I create so much anxiety for myself. It is unbearable. How can I solve this problem? How can I get past this ordeal? This is a tough fight to be battling with. It is a huge obstacle. I need to find a way to beat the odds. I must not be afraid so that I can live a better life.

5-6-10

How embarrassing. As I walked into the local coffee shop this morning, before entering I stopped and looked at the door handle to get in. I stared at it for a few seconds paralyzed and I knew that I could not touch it. Not today. Not with all the bacteria that the door handle possessed. To the right of the door there was a handicap button which when pushed automatically opens the door. I was able to push it but nothing happened. It was busted. The door remained shut. During this whole ordeal there was a man behind me trying to get into the coffee shop as well. I could only imagine what was going through his head. He must have been wondering why a physically able human was just standing there repetitively pushing the handicap button refusing to open the door the way a normal able-bodied human does. Finally the man behind me went in front and opened the door for both of us. I politely thanked the gentleman. This is the story of my life.

Another issue which has been affecting my life negatively occurred earlier this morning as well. As you already know I am on several medications for my OCD and depression so I must go to the pharmacy quite often. The issue is that upon receiving your medication you must write down your signature with a communal pen. This is a pharmacy. This is where ill, contagious people go to pick up their medication and we all must share the same pen. This really bothers me. The pen must be contaminated. Obviously it is. So now every time I pick up my medication from the pharmacy and sign my name with the contaminated, communal pen I must then go home and compulsively wash my hands. I find this very annoying and I need to overcome this issue.

5-6-10

Once it has you the trap is set. You feel powerless to the obsessive-compulsive disorder. It takes you away to a dark place you never want to end up in. Everything that you taught yourself is suddenly erased. The door out seems locked. You are stuck performing the rituals to a very obsessive degree. There is nothing you can do now. No convincing of any kind will break the spell. You try to pull away but cannot. The grip of the OCD is far too tight. It sucks you back in. Time and time again. This is the cycle. This is the routine. But it does not have to be this way. I need to train my brain not to allow it. This hell. To often am I trapped in the *suffer cycle*. I must practice breaking free. When I am trapped how can I climb my way out to freedom? How can I breathe free? Life is too short for this tragic game. It is a game that fills me with shame. So I will learn to break free. I cannot tolerate this self-inflicted punishment any longer. It is killing me. It is tearing me apart. Learn to walk away from the trap. Learn to walk away from the suffering. Remember, the pain of resisting the obsessive-compulsive disorder is a good pain. The pain of giving in to the obsessive-compulsive disorder is a bad pain. Make the decision. Make the right choice. I must take control. Despite its biological influence and stronghold, obsessive-compulsive disorder can be beaten. Destroy the urge to constantly give in. Destroy the demon…

5-9-10

I am so depressed and lonely. I am on an emotional rollercoaster ride. Besides my OCD lies this dark depression. It eats away at me. I do not know why it haunts me so. I wish I did not feel this low. It is not always. It is right now though. I want to feel good, healthy, and alive. I do not like living in this darkness. It scares me so much. I wish the torment and agony would go away. It feels horrid. I am so worried about what to do with my life. I have no prospects for a career and I am getting older quickly. What do I do? Where do I turn to for help? Praying helps. I will continue to pray.

5-23-10

I am freaking out. My anxiety is very high these days and I feel sadder than usual. I drank a lot of beers last night so I feel that this is the reason for my sadness. My body is probably craving more escape. With mental illness comes substance abuse. Mental illness is extremely painful so to cope I sometimes use drugs. Drugs, which include alcohol, serve as an escape and believe me; I am often looking for an escape. A way out. I am always looking to get away from my madness but the search is always unsuccessful. My dissatisfaction with my life only creates more chaos and anxiety. My dissatisfaction with life feeds my depression. It is quite horrible.

Positive thinking seems so unrealistic right now. I want to be and remain positive but I am feeling trapped in a hole unfortunately. Climbing out does not seem realistic right now either. Even if I manage to climb out I would not know where to go. Well I say this now, but once I climb out of the hole I am sure I will know where to go. I can't put my finger on why I am feeling so low. Is it because there is not enough certainty in my life right now? The only certainty I do have is that I will wake up mentally ill which aggravates and depresses me. I know that there are so many souls out there suffering as well. I wish that there was some miracle out there to heal our minds; to heal our souls. I need a magic potion to stop the insanity. The medication which I do take daily certainly is not doing the trick. I am sure I would be worse off without it but it simply is not enough. It does not ease the burden to the point where I feel satisfied with who I am and what my life is about.

6-1-10

I wish so badly that I was not afflicted with OCD. It really takes all the fun out of life. But I guess without suffering, one cannot truly grow.

6-7-10

I am trying so desperately to make something of myself. I feel that my writing is all I have but I fear it may be meaningless at the same time. All I write about is OCD. It is all my life. OCD. I am constantly trying to figure out ways to combat the disease. It is wearing me down and I feel hopeless. I feel that I am stuck with it for the rest of my days. I am so obsessed with my obsessive-compulsive disorder. It is eating a hole in my heart. It aches. It kills. I am often sitting alone trying to figure out a way to destroy the demon but constantly thinking about the demon maybe a bad idea. Essentially, you are what you think, and so if I am constantly thinking about OCD then OCD is all that I am allowing myself to be. The demon is all I am.

I am so worried that this book of mine is not enough. That it will not reach anyone. I fear it is a waste. I am terrified that my written words are a waste of my time and that of the reader's. I dream that my written words can change something. Whether it be my life or the life of another. I do have aspiration with this book. I want it to touch lives. That would give me a feeling of success and self worth. If not, I am then not sure what I will do. Maybe keep writing and try again. It is just so hard to write down anything that is profound enough to touch another's life. After all, I am just a man. I do not have the answers. I am full of questions and doubt.

What more can I say today that I have not already touched upon. I am terrified of upcoming life events. Tomorrow I am going on a beach trip with friends but the problem is that I am a creature of habit. I am uncomfortable being a guest at a home which is not mine. When one struggles with routine OCD, it is very hard to pack up and take a break from the routines. I know that it will probably be good for me to take a vacation from myself and my obsessive-compulsive routine lifestyle, but it is creating so much anxiety, worry, pain, and frustration. What can I do? I cannot stay calm. I am freaking out! I want to stay within my comfort zone so badly. I need help from God to get through this obstacle.

It is funny that to most people a beach trip creates a feeling of joy and relaxation but for me it creates a feeling of dread and misery. Clearly I am on a wrong path. This I know and am aware of. But what can I do to change this? I do not know. All I can do right now is be patient and strong. I must ignore the anxiety and pain of the upcoming events and stay strong. Strong enough to get to the beach and at least try to enjoy it. Little obstacles frighten me to a maximum level. I really need to become tougher mentally, spiritually, and emotionally.

All I do is attempt to fight, fight, fight. I need to begin to accept, accept, accept. I have got to take the pain of the present moment and sit with it. Whether it dissipates or not, I must accept the pain. I must be brave. Living with obsessive-compulsive disorder is so very complicated. My words still do not do it justice.

6-13-10

I am a bit more depressed today than usual. Maybe it has to do with the lack of sunlight that has been affecting the Boston area for the last few days. Maybe I have the Sunday blues. I am looking forward to the Celtics vs. Lakers championship game tonight. Should be fun. I am really depressed because life is so complex and hard to get through. Everyday is so permanently hard yet the time of the day is so fleeting. My life is passing right by me and I am struggling in my consciousness; crippled by anxiety, stress, and nervousness about the days to come. I still am unable to live for today only.

I did make it to the beach this past week but I did not enjoy it the way it was meant to be enjoyed. My anxiety there was so high that I left a day early. I took an expensive bus ride home by myself. The reason I had to leave so early was that being forced out of my regular OCD routine had created too much internal pain for my psyche. I had to escape back to my normality which is hell in its own right. I left hell to come back to hell essentially.

I do not even want to be writing right now. I feel too numb. I am not writing with passion because I am not writing positively. I am stuck in uncertainty, inaction, indecision, and with disdain. This is not who I want to be. This is not the life for me.

6-14-10

Clearly the hardest part of my day, the hardest part of my life, is to simply get my depressed self out of bed. I lie there knowing the hell that waits. OCD has me really beaten right now. Beat to the point where I am scared to begin my life each and every opportunity that I have. Today I fought extra hard just to get myself out of bed before noon which happens to be an early rise for me. I remember lying there waiting for myself to develop the energy to face the upcoming life events. Working out, brushing my teeth, taking a brutal *power shower.* Finally after torturing myself for hours I gained the strength to rise. I accomplished what I set out to accomplish but as expected it was painful. I did accomplish however, painful as it may have seemed.

After an anxiety provoked late mourning prep for the day I was then ready to get the hell out of my apartment which is more like a torture chamber of depression. Luckily one of my best friends gave me a ring on the telephone. To his surprise I actually picked up which I am not expected to do before about four o'clock. My friend understands how hard my mornings are. This is why I trust him as a friend. Shortly there after my friend and I met up for coffee and food which was pleasant. Now we are sitting in the local coffee shop. I am attempting to enjoy myself but it remains to be challenging. But hey, again, life is meant to be challenging.

6-15-10

So I am still suffering from extreme mental anguish but so what…Life is meant to be enjoyed but at the same time it is a very challenging ride. To beat this demon I need to stop concentrating on how bad life is but rather focus on how good it is behind the façade of hell. This is very difficult. Life is an illusion. It grips you and makes you feel horrible but I know that underneath there is a glowing light. A sense of calm. Something that cannot be fully explained but only fully experienced. Some lasting joy is attainable. It must be. Hardship is part of this lasting joy. Joy cannot be permanent but it may remain in one's life if one allows it to do so. This is how I need to live my life. I need to breathe this belief that there is a glowing light underneath this existence of hell that I have grown so accustomed to.

Without these struggles of mine how would I be able to call myself a man? A man must suffer. Suffering builds strong character. This is undeniable. I will not loose sight of this. I have spent so much time searching for ways to avoid the suffering and never realized how important the suffering really is. All the self help books and guru dependence that I have fallen prey to serve a purpose for some but not for me. Eternal bliss is not a part of my life right now and probably never will be until maybe the day I die. I have been falsely searching for this idea of eternal bliss but am now happy to finally understand that it does not exist in this life. Suffering is the answer. We all must suffer to become better and wiser; both men and women. I can find some peace in this thought. Suffering is my new serenity. It is a part of me that has not disappeared through out all of my existence, so why am I trying to run away from it so hard. I must embrace this suffering. I must embrace this pain. I must embrace this life!

7-18-10

I have not written in quite some time now. The reason for this is fear. I really do not know what to write anymore. I am so terrified by my future. I feel that I have no prospects and nothing to offer society mainly because of my debilitating mental condition. The only real comfort I truly have is putting down my thoughts in written form so that they may be shared by and with others who maybe care. To feel that you have nothing to offer and nothing positive ahead is an awful dilemma to create for one's own self. Hopelessness. This is a dilemma that is not withering away unfortunately. I want to feel positive about my future but how can I when I feel so out of control. I want a release from this negativity and pain. I dream of a way out. I dream of a life where I am not frightened by tomorrow. God help me! I would like to stay still and look at the perfect sky without distraction from all the forces against me. The stressors of day to day living are always hindering my ability to truly enjoy life. These stressors and obstacles are killing me. I want to ignore them but cannot. My life is radically consumed with these stressors. Obsessive-compulsive disorder allows minor and simple stressors to grow into agonizing obstacles that seem insurmountable. How to fight this I do not know anymore. Time passes and I continue to worry. Life goes on but I stay behind. Suffering. But then again, I said it myself. To live well one must embrace suffering.

8-31-10

Life must go on. I am now learning to embrace the suffering step by step. Each day I am gaining new battle strategies in winning the war against OCD and depression. I will succeed. I am practicing positive thinking and it is working. I am applying myself and am using my strengths. This is what I have been waiting for. I am breaking down the walls. Even if the suffering continues it will no longer discourage me from gaining empowerment. I will never quit. Positive changes are occurring. My weaknesses are dissolving. I am happy. With hard work a lot can change in a month. I have a long way to go but I will enjoy the journey.

9-7-10

I find myself in continuous prayer. It is a tool that I have been using to get myself through the hard points of living. Life is becoming better; however I am still struggling with obsessive-compulsive disorder, major anxiety, and depression. What I am doing to battle this negativity is performing the act of prayer. For me, it is a form of meditation. When I am in prayer my anxiety dissipates tremendously. My depression withers away. I strongly recommend prayer to battle OCD, anxiety, depression, or any other mental anguish. Whether or not you believe in God, you can still pray. You can pray to the unknown. We all have the freedom to do so. When in prayer, my OCD remains to sit on the side. I expect it to come back always, but sometimes I simply pray that it will disappear. I am aware of how simplistic and obvious this all sounds. "Pray to feel better." But it is in reality very special and a very intricate form of meditation. It is a special tool to relieve a worried mind. Prayer is a necessary tool in my war against mental illness. Sometimes I pray for nothing. I simply lie or sit devoted to the power that be. Often I pray for loved ones' wellbeing. When in pain, I pray that I will be able to conquer my demons. Sometimes I pray by simply giving thanks for the gift of life. It really does not matter what I am praying for as long as I am in patient prayer. It helps me. It is an effective way to re-train my brain; to change the way my mind functions. Praying gives a mentally ill man hope when hope is so hard to come by. It serves as a break from the hurting. I want all who suffer to at least give prayer a chance. I am giving prayer a chance and it is helping to change my reality. Some who doubt faith will obviously doubt prayer as well. But I am passionate in my belief that 'prayer' and 'the devotion to a specific religion or God' do not have to co-exist. You can doubt God. You can doubt religion. You can doubt faith. This is acceptable. But I believe that prayer can still be used as a tool in battling mental illness even with all the doubt surrounding it.

When one is in prayer, he or she does not have to pray outside of themselves. I find that to pray I must do so 'within myself.' My doubt can serve as a weapon towards success, as strange as that sounds. If you suffer from mental illness or discomfort it is very easy to doubt a higher power. However, I assure you that this is okay. It is fine to doubt a higher power. Within this uncertainty of a higher power there comes room for prayer. Trust me! Embrace this uncertainty. The uncertainty can serve as a blessing in disguise. Uncertainty opens up a whole world of possibility. To be honest, I cannot be sure that God exists but it is my lack of understanding which gives me faith. There is no one correct way to pray, but I choose to pray with uncertainty. I pray with a lack of understanding. I pray as a human being. This is in fact what makes the prayer so intense. Not only am I looking within myself, but because I am relying on uncertainty while in prayer, I am also outside of myself at the same time. It really is brilliant. Pray with doubt. Pray with uncertainty. This is not a problem or an incorrect form of prayer. It is a useful skill and tool.

As I write these words I realize just how uncertain I am of this higher power I choose to call GOD. To my surprise, this is an empowering and comforting feeling. If I am uncertain of the existence of God then I am also uncertain of what my praying to God can actually accomplish. In other words, because I do not know for sure that God exists I also do not know for sure what God can give. If I pray to God within my own self I am uncertain of what the results of the praying will be and what the praying is actually accomplishing for me. I find this magnificent because it opens up the door to hope. I have no proof of a higher power. Proof of such an idea is incomprehensible. The beauty of this however is that I also have no proof that my prayers will go unanswered. This is glorious freedom. I can pray unaware of what the praying holds for me. I can pray with uncertainty and feel good and confident about my prayers at the same time. There are no answers to the question concerning the existence of God. God is an idea that I hold dear to my heart. But because I do not know for sure what God truly is, I do not know for sure what my praying is doing for me other than giving me momentary peace. The prayers I meditate on may be saving my life. They may be saving my existence. I do not need to know. You and I can be uncertain together. However, what I do know is that while I am uncertain when in prayer, I do feel comforted 'in the now' and 'in the present moment.' This comfort I am blessed to feel in the moments of prayer allows me to have hope that within myself there is something amazing. Within myself there is something unexplainable and I am content to be uncertain of it. One can pray without limits. Certain or uncertain, you are in prayer. Your mind is adjusting to the sacred act and your life is becoming more valuable.

9-8-10

Life is so beautiful. I am realizing this now. With age comes wisdom. With wisdom comes appreciation. For so long I have been letting my mental disease take away life's beautiful glory. Now I am taking that glory back and am living with it. My soul is alive. I can feel it. I am breathing free. Life gives us so much opportunity and I refuse to turn my back on this opportunity because of my OCD. My mental condition will no longer dictate my life and my emotions. I am strong now and ready to win this war! It has been quite the long journey and the journey never ends. Possibilities are limitless and for the first time I am seeing these possibilities as positive; not negative. I have gained a new found sense of optimism and I love it! I am finally excited to be living. Whether or not the OCD remains, I will be sure to battle it. If the suffering continues I will embrace it and grow stronger from it. I will learn from it. We are all evolving human beings every moment of our lives. Treasure this fact. Do not waste it. Each moment is a new opportunity for discovery and joy. Let this joy last.